MAYWOOD PUBLIC LIBRARY

W9-CER-124

MAYWOOD PUBLIC LIBRARY
121 SOUTH 5TH AVE
MAYWOOD, IL 60153

Drug Trafficking

Drug Trafficking

Other books in the Current Controversies series:

Drug Trafficking

Auriana Ojeda, *Book Editor*

Daniel Leone, *President*
Bonnie Szumski, *Publisher*
Scott Barbour, *Managing Editor*

CURRENT CONTROVERSIES

No part of this book may be reproduced or used in any form or by any means, electrical, mechanical, or otherwise, including, but not limited to, photocopy, recording, or any information storage and retrieval system, without prior written permission from the publisher.

Cover photo: © Reuters NewMedia Inc./Corbis

Library of Congress Cataloging-in-Publication Data

Drug trafficking / Auriana Ojeda, book editor.
    p. cm. — (Current controversies)
    Includes bibliographical references and index.
    ISBN 0-7377-0854-9 (pbk. : alk. paper) — ISBN 0-7377-0855-7
(lib. : alk. paper)
    1. Narcotics, Control of—United States. 2. Drug traffic—United
States. I. Ojeda, Auriana, 1977– II. Series.

HV5825 .D77688   2002
363.45'0973—dc21

2001040122
CIP

© 2002 by Greenhaven Press, Inc., PO Box 289009, San Diego, CA 92198-9009
Printed in the U.S.A.

Every effort has been made to trace the owners of copyrighted material.

Contents

No: The War on Drugs Is a Failure

Chapter 2: What Are the Effects of Drug Trafficking?

Chapter 3: Can International Assistance to Colombia Combat Drug Trafficking?

Yes: International Assistance to Colombia Is Necessary to Combat Drug Trafficking

Chapter 4: How Can Drug Trafficking Be Combated?

Foreword

By definition, controversies are "discussions of questions in which opposing opinions clash" (Webster's Twentieth Century Dictionary Unabridged). Few would deny that controversies are a pervasive part of the human condition and exist on virtually every level of human enterprise. Controversies transpire between individuals and among groups, within nations and between nations. Controversies supply the grist necessary for progress by providing challenges and challengers to the status quo. They also create atmospheres where strife and warfare can flourish. A world without controversies would be a peaceful world; but it also would be, by and large, static and prosaic.

The Series' Purpose

The purpose of the Current Controversies series is to explore many of the social, political, and economic controversies dominating the national and international scenes today. Titles selected for inclusion in the series are highly focused and specific. For example, from the larger category of criminal justice, Current Controversies deals with specific topics such as police brutality, gun control, white collar crime, and others. The debates in Current Controversies also are presented in a useful, timeless fashion. Articles and book excerpts included in each title are selected if they contribute valuable, long-range ideas to the overall debate. And wherever possible, current information is enhanced with historical documents and other relevant materials. Thus, while individual titles are current in focus, every effort is made to ensure that they will not become quickly outdated. Books in the Current Controversies series will remain important resources for librarians, teachers, and students for many years.

In addition to keeping the titles focused and specific, great care is taken in the editorial format of each book in the series. Book introductions and chapter prefaces are offered to provide background material for readers. Chapters are organized around several key questions that are answered with diverse opinions representing all points on the political spectrum. Materials in each chapter include opinions in which authors clearly disagree as well as alternative opinions in which authors may agree on a broader issue but disagree on the possible solutions. In this way, the content of each volume in Current Controversies mirrors the mosaic of opinions encountered in society. Readers will quickly realize that there are many viable answers to these complex issues. By questioning each author's conclusions, students and casual readers can begin to develop the critical thinking skills so important to evaluating opinionated material.

Current Controversies is also ideal for controlled research. Each anthology in the series is composed of primary sources taken from a wide gamut of informational categories including periodicals, newspapers, books, United States and foreign government documents, and the publications of private and public organizations. Readers will find factual support for reports, debates, and research papers covering all areas of important issues. In addition, an annotated table of contents, an index, a book and periodical bibliography, and a list of organizations to contact are included in each book to expedite further research.

Perhaps more than ever before in history, people are confronted with diverse and contradictory information. During the Persian Gulf War, for example, the public was not only treated to minute-to-minute coverage of the war, it was also inundated with critiques of the coverage and countless analyses of the factors motivating U.S. involvement. Being able to sort through the plethora of opinions accompanying today's major issues, and to draw one's own conclusions, can be a complicated and frustrating struggle. It is the editors' hope that Current Controversies will help readers with this struggle.

Greenhaven Press anthologies primarily consist of previously published material taken from a variety of sources, including periodicals, books, scholarly journals, newspapers, government documents, and position papers from private and public organizations. These original sources are often edited for length and to ensure their accessibility for a young adult audience. The anthology editors also change the original titles of these works in order to clearly present the main thesis of each viewpoint and to explicitly indicate the opinion presented in the viewpoint. These alterations are made in consideration of both the reading and comprehension levels of a young adult audience. Every effort is made to ensure that Greenhaven Press accurately reflects the original intent of the authors included in this anthology.

"The international drug trade is estimated to generate $300 billion to $400 billion annually."

Introduction

In the 2000 film *Traffic*, Robert Wakefield is a superior court judge newly appointed to head the Office of National Drug Control Policy (ONDCP). In one scene, Wakefield compliments the outgoing drug czar on his successes, only to receive a quizzical look and a resigned reply: "I'm not sure I made the slightest difference."

Such is the sentiment of much of society concerning the war on drugs and drug trafficking in the United States. Many argue that the war on drugs costs America far too much in tax dollars, law enforcement effort, and people's lives, and that, despite an overwhelming effort, little progress has been made. The drug control budget in the United States has increased from $9.7 billion in 1990 to $17.7 billion in 2000. The Drug Enforcement Administration (DEA) increased its number of agents from 3,191 in 1990 to 4,561 in 2000. In spite of these increases, the number of drug users increased from 5.8 percent of the population in 1992 to 6.7 percent in 1998. In 1999 an estimated 14.8 million Americans were current users of illegal drugs, and there were approximately 208,000 users of heroin, more than triple the 1993 figure of 68,000. Drug use in America has steadily risen in the last ten years despite increases in law enforcement efforts, budgets, and staffing.

In 1968 Richard Nixon coined the phrase "war on drugs" to describe America's efforts to battle the production, distribution, and use of illegal drugs. In 1972 Nixon combined four government agencies dedicated to combating drugs to create the DEA. In the 1980s, Ronald Reagan revived the war on drugs and increased the efforts of the DEA to reduce the supply of drugs entering the United States. Reagan initiated a series of laws allowing federal officials to access military intelligence, training, and equipment to track and intercept drug traffickers. Around the same time, federal and local governments passed laws allowing property and assets derived from drug profits to be confiscated and retained by officials. Under the Reagan administration, drug treatment and education programs were initiated, including Nancy Reagan's "Just Say No" campaign in which children were encouraged by media messages and slogans to resist offers of drugs.

The increase in law enforcement efforts was intended to reduce drug trafficking by enacting more severe legal sanctions for convicted drug dealers, but the enormity of profits to be made from smuggling and selling drugs overrides the threat of punishment. The international drug trade is estimated to generate $300 billion to $400 billion annually. Such a large profit not only provides a strong incentive to sell drugs, but also allows criminals greater access to technological advantages. Because the traffickers have a higher budget than drug enforcement officers do, they are able to develop more sophisticated means of producing, transporting, and hiding their drugs. According to journalists John Ward Anderson and William Branigin, "In recent years, drug mafias have bought commercial jetliners and built a fleet of two-man submarines to move drugs to the United States. They have secreted loads in propane tanks and containers of hazardous materials, in small cans of tuna fish and five-gallon drums of jalapeño peppers. One trafficking group fashioned a special mold that was used to successfully ship cocaine from Mexico through the United States and into Canada completely sealed inside the walls of porcelain toilets." The existing budget to fight the supply of drugs cannot compete with the limitless resources available to drug traffickers.

Critics of the drug war argue that the amount of money spent on unsuccessfully reducing the supply of drugs would be better used to fight the enormous demand for drugs in the United States. To accomplish this, many favor drug prevention education programs that strive to deter children from experimenting with drugs. They speak favorably of the "Just Say No" campaign of the Reagan administration, which launched the "This is your brain on drugs" commercials as well as posters with the slogan "Drugs Kill." They also support the current Drug Abuse Resistance Education (DARE) program, in which trained, uniformed police officers speak to classrooms about the negative consequences of drug use and teach children the skills to resist peer pressure and intimidation. Supporters of these programs contend that children are less likely to succumb to the dangers of drug use—and less likely to become drug-abusing adults—if they are informed about the risks.

In addition to drug education, proponents of the demand-reduction approach advocate increased funding for drug treatment programs. Treatment programs include various drug rehabilitation clinics and job support and training for rehabilitated drug addicts. Another form of treatment is the distribution of methadone to heroin addicts. Methadone is a synthetic opiate that blocks the craving for heroin and reduces the painful and debilitating withdrawal symptoms. According to Michael Massing, author of *The Fix*, a book about America's drug problem,

> Relying solely on drug-fighting efforts abroad, the government would have to spend $783 million more a year to reduce cocaine consumption by 1 percent; relying on interdiction, it would have to spend $366 million more, and on domestic law enforcement, $246 million. Relying solely on treatment, however, the government would have to spend only $34 million more to achieve that 1 percent reduction. In other words [according to a 1994 RAND study], treatment was seven times more cost-effective than local law enforcement, ten times more effective than interdiction, and twenty-three times more effective than attacking drugs at their source.

Massing and others maintain that drug treatment is not only more effective at reducing drug use than interdiction efforts, but also more cost effective for American taxpayers.

Others contend that attacking the supply of drugs is essential to reduce drug use and the social ills it produces. According to talk-show host and syndicated columnist Oliver North, "The prevalence of so many drugs, in such astounding quantities and purity, results in extraordinary violence, corruption, and downright lawlessness here in the United States." North and others argue that the effort poured into drug interdiction and law enforcement is necessary to maintain the no-tolerance drug policy in the United States. Law enforcement seized $82 million worth of drugs in 1999, more than three times the 1990 figure of $24 million. The DEA argues that this increase in drug seizures demonstrates the effectiveness of supply reduction in the war on drugs.

Despite many arguments against America's war on drugs, the prevailing sentiment strongly advocates a no-tolerance drug policy. *Drug Trafficking: Current Controversies* offers perspectives on the various effects drug trafficking has on society and the efforts law enforcement and the government are making to combat it. While drug trafficking is seen as a transnational threat, attempts to eradicate it have caused much controversy in the United States.

Chapter 1

Can the War on Drugs Be Won?

CURRENT CONTROVERSIES

Chapter Preface

The term "war on drugs," coined in 1968 by Richard Nixon, describes the American public's intolerance of illegal drugs, drug users, and drug traffickers. Under this ethos, officials strive to eliminate drugs from society by enacting strict legal penalties for drug users, dealers, and smugglers.

Many argue that the war on drugs has been unsuccessful and should be abandoned. Despite spending millions of American tax dollars on drug interdiction efforts and the incarceration of nonviolent drug offenders, critics point out that the number of drug users in the United States increased from 5.8 percent of the population in 1992 to 6.7 percent in 1998.

Some opponents of the drug war argue that drugs should be legalized, freeing up money for more effective uses, such as providing more funding for treatment centers and antidrug education. According to retired army intelligence officer Patrick Lloyd Hatcher, "[Legalization] would immediately cut the foreign connection, since all drugs could be produced and marketed much more efficiently inside the United States itself. The U.S. government could then redirect its drug-fighting budget to education aimed at potential users and to succor the truly wounded of the war, the homegrown addicts of hard drugs."

Others argue that drug use is the most important problem facing society, as it not only harms the individuals who use drugs, but also damages their families, fosters violence, and increases the prevalence of blood-borne diseases such as HIV and hepatitis. As Barry McCaffrey, former director of the Office of National Drug Control Policy, claims, "a twelve-year-old smoking a joint [is] the most dangerous [thing] in America." McCaffrey also claims that the war on drugs has made remarkable progress: "Current drug policies are reducing drug use and its consequences. Drug use in this country declined by half [from] 1979 [to 1999]. The number of current users dropped from 25,000,000 in 1979 to 13,000,000 in 1996. The decrease in . . . use of cocaine [in 1999 is] even more dramatic." McCaffrey contends that the war on drugs is necessary to protect America's children and that legalization would harm American society.

Whether the war on drugs can solve society's drug problem is one of the issues debated in the following chapter.

The War on Drugs Can Be Won

by Newt Gingrich

About the author: *Newt Gingrich was the Speaker of the House of Representatives from 1995 to 1999 and served as a member of Congress for twenty years. He currently serves as a senior fellow at the American Enterprise Institute and as a distinguished visiting fellow at the Hoover Institution at Stanford University.*

The time has come for the drug war to enter a new, winnable stage. This is a war that has consumed the nation, with varying degrees of success, for nearly three decades. In the 1980s, following the leadership of Nancy Reagan and the effective, unequivocal "Just Say No" campaign, illegal drug use declined year after year.

In the '90s however, as the messages from the White House and the media became more ambiguous, drug use has increased—especially among the most vulnerable, our young people. We have reached a moment when a majority of all high school seniors admit they've tried an illegal drug. In 1992, 40.7 percent had used an illicit drug; by 1997, the number had jumped to 54.3 percent.

Today, the Republican Congress declares that we are as committed to creating a drug-free America as we were in passing the Contract With America three years ago. There is a simple yet essential reason for the intensity of our commitment: Unlike other conflicts in which this nation has been engaged, the war on drugs is at essence a comprehensive, all-out fight to protect our children.

Some people are convinced that the war cannot be won. The naysayers suggest that "It's all been done before" or "It's all been said before." However, these were many of the same people who threw up their hands when facing three decades of unbalanced budgets. They thought that the goal of a balanced budget was a fantasy. In 1994, Republicans ran on a contract that said, given the chance, we could make a balanced budget a reality. As a result, not only do we have a balanced budget, we now have a budget surplus.

The Republican Congress believes that legislative commitment combined

Reprinted from "Winning the War on Drugs," by Newt Gingrich, *The Washington Times*, weekly edition, May 4–10, 1998.

with the good will and efforts of the American people are a force that can rise to any challenge. Creating a drug-free America is a goal for a generation—a long-term focused strategy. It should be, must be, the number one priority of all concerned Americans. The war on drugs is ultimately a fight for our children: They are our future. Drug abuse is a modern day plague that tears apart families as it steals the innocence of youth. Without a coherent policy to protect them from the evils and devastation of drug abuse, we abandon them and put our country at risk.

> *"The war on drugs is at essence a comprehensive, all-out fight to protect our children."*

This campaign will be fought on three major fronts: Deterring demand; stopping supply; and increasing accountability.

Deterring Demand: Nine out of 10 people believe solving our drug crisis is an urgent issue. Yet, we must educate and further engage Americans on the nature of this problem. The deployment began with a vote April 30 on the Drug-Free America Blue Ribbon Campaign Resolution. It spells out clearly the extent of the drug problem and designates a week in September as Blue Ribbon Week. During this week, all Americans are encouraged to wear a blue ribbon to heighten awareness of the drug crisis and become volunteers in the fight for our children. In addition to the concrete legislative action to control the poisons flooding our streets, the American people must have the essential information to face this crisis.

The Drug-Free Workplaces Act will help small and medium businesses implement drug-free workplace programs that will enhance productivity and quality of life. The Drug-Free Congressional Leadership Resolution will strongly encourage all members of Congress to follow the lead of 76 of their colleagues who have created community anti-drug coalitions. We will build on our success with the Drug-Free Communities Act by doubling our investment at the local level to $20 million.

Stopping Supply: Americans clearly see interdiction as the top priority foreign policy issue, a higher priority than either illegal immigration or terrorism. Responding to that concern the Congress will pass the Drug-Free Borders Act that establishes severe criminal penalties for those who use violence against customs officers at our borders. It increases the penalties for making false statements when declaring goods into the U.S. The Drug-Free Hemisphere Act will authorize the creation of international law enforcement academies, allowing U.S. law enforcement to train anti-drug police abroad, and also authorizes non-lethal counter-narcotic assistance abroad.

Increasing Accountability: Accountability must start at the top. Federal, state and local agencies must be empowered to win the war on drugs and be held accountable for their actions. The American people must have greater information to judge for themselves how well the fight for their children is going. Thus, for the first time in history, federal funding will be tied to specific drug reduction goals set by Congress. The targets include reducing nationwide drug use by more than 50 percent by 2002 to reducing the percentage of all Americans using drugs from today's figure of 6.1 percent to less than 3 percent. This measure will require greater coordination of efforts among the 54 federal agencies receiving anti-drug funding and so will give the drug czar oversight of all of them.

The Republican Congress and the Speaker's Task Force for A Drug-Free America believe that these and other anti-drug measures we will vote on this spring are, collectively, the most significant pieces of legislation that Congress has considered since the Contract With America. Drugs themselves are "gateways" to so many other societal ills: violent crime, spousal and child abuse, and sexual assault. If we care about our children and about ourselves, there cannot be a more important undertaking for the future.

This is not some pipe dream. We can win the war on drugs. We can save our children. The American people demand it. Congress is committed to it. Our young people deserve it. We now ask only that the president and the administration pledge their unequivocal support.

America Must Continue the War on Drugs

by Barry McCaffrey

About the author: *Barry McCaffrey served as the director of the Office of National Drug Control Policy from 1996 to 2001.*

Recent calls for legalization as the panacea for the nation's drug ills should be taken with the salt of history. The tendency to forget much of America's experience with addictive substances goes to the very nature of drugs and the culture they spawn. A drugged society suffers from long-term memory loss to the point of amnesia.

The lure of illegal drugs involves a desire for intense pleasure and instant reward. Drug users crave out-of-body joy and peace at the drop of a pill, in a few breaths, or within minutes of injection. Lost in the self and the present, the person on drugs is neither preparing for the future nor learning from the past. The drug culture nods in the "now"; its orientation is ahistorical. Yet history has much to teach us about the problems of substance abuse, which we ignore at our peril.

America's confrontation with dangerous drugs dates back to the 19th century when over-the-counter syrups were heavily laced with morphine; Coca-Cola and other beverages contained cocaine; and Bayer Pharmaceutical Products introduced heroin—touted as "non-addictive" and sold without prescription (one year before Bayer offered aspirin). At the turn of the century, opium dens catered to communities throughout the United States.

We do not have to speculate about what would happen if addictive drugs were legal without prescription. Our country already tried that route, suffered, and roundly rejected the scourge of drugs on our communities, schools, workplaces and families.

By popular demand, the Food and Drug Act of 1906 required that all ingredients in products and medicines be revealed to consumers, many of whom had become addicted to substances falsely marketed as safe.

In 1909, the Smoking Opium Exclusion Act banned the importation of smok-

Reprinted from "Getting a Fix on U.S. Drug Use History," by Barry McCaffrey, *The Washington Times*, March 16, 1997.

able opium—providing the first national anti-drug legislation. Five years later, the Harrison Narcotic Act implemented even broader and more effective drug control laws. In 1911, the first International Conference on Opium convened in The Hague to control narcotics trafficking. By the 1920s, doctors in America were prohibited from prescribing opiates for nonmedical purposes, including the treatment of addicts.

Problems with cocaine addiction plagued Hollywood in the '20s to the point where movie mogul Louis B. Mayer complained: "If this keeps up, there won't be any motion picture industry."

In response to popular outrage over depictions of drug use in film, 37 states passed censorship bills by 1922. The drug problem did not first hit the United States in the 1960s, as is often thought. An earlier drug epidemic raged between 1885 and 1925, followed by a resurgence from 1950 to 1970 when heroin poured into America from Turkey by way of France. Ten years later, a third and incredibly destructive wave of drug abuse brought havoc to our shores as Colombian cartels flooded our streets with cocaine.

The tendency to underestimate the hazards of drug use has been made in successive generations. We forget what has been painfully demonstrated in years past. The seductive quality of drugs fooled many professionals and laymen. The father of modern psychiatry, Sigmund Freud, initially thought cocaine was non-addictive and relatively harmless—a mistake made in the mid-1880s that was repeated nearly a hundred years later. Leading universities hosted professors infatuated with psychedelics in the 1960s and '70s or stimulants and narcotics in the '80s and '90s.

Many physicians and researchers grossly underestimated drug dangers. Dr. Morris Manges of Mount Sinai Hospital wrote, in an 1898 issue of the *New York Medical Journal,* about treating coughs with heroin: "apparently, there was no habituation to the drug." By 1900, Dr. Manges released a second glowing report for heroin based on a survey of 141 doctors. The author noted only a small number of cases where addiction was observed. But three years later, Dr. George Pettey voiced unequivocal alarm in "The Heroin Habit: Another Curse," published in the *Alabama Medical Journal.* Dr. Pettey realized that heroin produced "what is for all intents and purposes the opium habit!"

With respect to cocaine, the absence of heroin-type withdrawal symptoms tricked some researchers into missing this drug's addictive quality, which is based on reward, according to Dr. Robert Dupont, a former head of the National Institute of Drug Abuse. In 1979, Dr. Robert Byck of Yale Medical School warned about the devastation caused by smoked coca paste used in Peru—this before crack ominously captured so many Americans.

> *"Drug use is not limited to one area of the country or social class but permeates suburban and rural areas as well as urban locations."*

Wooed into a false sense of security by the supposed benign quality of smoked marijuana, unwitting victims of crack cocaine wrongly concluded that smoking this substance—unlike injecting it—would be a safe route of administration. (Dr. David Musto highlights a parallel misconception a century earlier when physicians and patients alike mistakenly concluded that the use of a syringe with pure morphine, which reduced the quantity of drugs needed to produce the same effect, would limit rather than expand the likelihood of addiction.)

Actually, crack cocaine made heroin "look like the good old days," according to historian Dr. Jill Jonnes. The advent of crack houses and crack babies (the NIDA National Pregnancy and Health Survey estimated 1.5 percent to 2 percent of American infants in 1992 had been exposed to cocaine in utero) marked a new and terrible stage in the history of drug abuse.

In 1986—the same year the military reported cutting drug use by half—the deaths of basketball star Len Bias and football star Don Rogers demonstrated to the public that one dose of cocaine could prove lethal even to healthy young athletes. Had anyone bothered to consult the research, they would have discovered that this fatal syndrome was identified decades ago. In addition, the historical experience of cultures as different as China, Egypt and Japan confirmed that no society could prosper while tolerating addictive drugs.

> *"Illegal drugs are a byproduct of an industrial society that has led us to tamper . . . with the body's inner environment."*

Drug use cannot be considered in a vacuum. We must understand it within the context of crime, violence, corruption, prostitution, multinational cartels, adverse health consequences, enormous social costs, and the collapse of our cities. Drug use is not limited to one area of the country or social class but permeates suburban and rural areas as well as urban locations.

On an international scale, narco-terrorists use the illegal drug trade as a means to other ends. Arms deals fueled by drug capital are part of the deal. On the other side of the drug register are young consumers. Youths are particularly vulnerable to the allure of drugs and to the damage toxic substances cause developing bodies and minds.

The drug problem has personal, psychological dimensions, but it is also a social, medical, communal, economic, and global problem that involves larger systems—beginning with the family and reaching to the nation and hemisphere.

America always has been a forward-thinking, optimistic country oriented toward the present and future. In an age of electronic communication and computers, instant transmission of information compounds the tendency to value what is news right now as opposed to yesterday. But ignorance of the past condemns us to repeat errors unnecessarily. An antidote to arrogance, memory is the key to education and collective progress. The history of illegal drugs informs the present.

Drug Trafficking

Illegal drugs are a byproduct of an industrial society that has led us to tamper—for better and for worse—with the body's inner environment. The United States has one of the worst addiction problems of any country in the developed world in part because of our wealth. Now we must focus our resources, including the intelligence of our greatest minds, to solve this problem.

We can lead the world in controlling illegal drugs—primarily through prevention and treatment—just as we made great strides in guarding consumer safety and cleaning up the outer environment. From seat belts to sewage disposal, America has used the law to protect citizens. The ill-termed "war on drugs" is another such effort. We must free all people besieged by the tyranny of drug dependence.

The Prohibition Strategy Can Win the War on Drugs

by the Office of National Drug Control Policy

About the author: *The Office of National Drug Control Policy is a branch of government dedicated to fighting drugs and drug traffickers.*

The first duty of government is to protect its citizens. The Constitution of the United States—as interpreted over 208 years—articulates the obligation of the federal government to uphold the public good, providing a bulwark against all threats, foreign and domestic. Illegal drugs constitute one such threat. Toxic, addictive substances present a hazard to society as a whole. Like a corrosive, insidious cancer, drug abuse diminishes the potential of our citizens for full growth and development.

The traditions of American government and democracy affirm self-determination and freedom. While government must minimize interference in the private lives of citizens, it cannot deny security to individuals and the collective culture the people uphold. Drug abuse and its consequences destroy personal liberty and the well-being of communities. Crime, violence, anti-social behavior, accidents, unintended pregnancies, drug-exposed infants, and addiction are only part of the price illegal drug use imposes on society. Every drug user risks his ability to think rationally and his potential for a full, productive life. Drug abuse drains the physical and moral strength of America. It spawns global criminal syndicates and bankrolls those who sell drugs to children. Illegal drugs foster crime and violence in our inner cities, suburbs, and rural areas.

Drug-induced deaths increased 47 percent between 1990 and 1994 and number approximately 14,000 a year. Illegal drugs also burden our society with approximately $67 billion in social, health, and criminal costs each year. Absent effective government action, the damage to our country would be even greater. Historians have documented America's experience with addictive drugs over the past two hundred years. The ebb and flow of drug use recurred in roughly thirty-year cycles: an uninformed or forgetful public becomes indifferent to the dangers of rising drug use only to recoil at its devastating consequences. . . .

Excerpted from "Drug Strategy: Overview," in part I of the Office of National Drug Control Policy's publication *National Drug Control Strategy*, February 1997.

Evolution of the National Drug Control Strategy

The Controlled Substances Act, Title II of the Comprehensive Drug Abuse Prevention and Control Act of 1970, is the legal foundation of the government's fight against abuse of drugs and other substances. This law consolidates numerous regulations pertaining to the manufacture and distribution of narcotics, stimulants, depressants, hallucinogens, anabolic steroids, and chemicals used in the illicit production of controlled substances.

The federal Anti-Drug Abuse Act of 1988 established as a policy goal of the United States government the creation of a drug-free America. A key provision of that act was the establishment of the Office of National Drug Policy to set priorities and objectives for national drug control, promulgate the *National Drug Control Strat*egy on an annual basis, and oversee the strategy's implementation. Congress requires that the strategy be comprehensive and research-based; contain long-range goals and shorter-term, measurable objectives; and seek to reduce drug abuse and its consequences. Specifically, drug abuse is likely to be curbed by: reducing the number of illegal drug users; preventing use of illegal drugs, alcohol, and tobacco by underage youth; and reducing the availability of illegal drugs. . . .

Since passage of the Anti-Drug Abuse Act, seven formal versions of the *National Drug Control Strategy* have been drafted. All defined the re-

> *"Like a corrosive, insidious cancer, drug abuse diminishes the potential of our citizens for full growth and development."*

duction in demand for illegal drugs as a main focus of drug control efforts. In addition, the documents soon recognized the prevention of drug, alcohol, and tobacco use among youth as the most important goal. The various strategies realized that no single approach could rescue the nation from the cycle of drug abuse. A consensus was reached that drug prevention, education, and treatment must be complemented by drug supply reduction abroad, on our borders, and within the United States. Each strategy also shared the commitment to maintain and enforce anti-drug laws. Finally, these strategies tied policy to an increasingly scientific, research-based body of knowledge about the nation's drug problems. . . .

Challenging Drug Abuse

Our nation's domestic challenge is to reduce drug use and its consequences while protecting individual liberties. Our international challenge is to develop effective programs that reduce the cultivation, production, and trafficking of illegal drugs while supporting democratic governance and human rights. . . .

Reducing the drug problem in America requires a multi-faceted, balanced program. We cannot hope to decrease drug abuse by relying exclusively on one approach. William Bennett laid out in the *1989 National Drug Control Strategy* a lesson that still applies today: ". . . no single tactic—pursued alone or to the detriment of other possible and valuable initiatives—can work to contain or reduce drug use." We can expect no panacea, no "silver bullet." We can neither arrest nor educate our way out of this problem. . . .

There can be no short-term solutions to a problem that requires education of each generation and resolute opposition to criminal traffickers. Our approach must be long-term and continuous. We will marshal the resources to resist drug traffickers, manage the social trauma of drug abuse, and create the engaged, supportive, community environment needed to educate American youth. . . .

One consequence of modern communication and transportation is a "shrinking" of the world and the nation. Drug abuse is not limited to one region of the country or one country in the world. [We must] use initiatives like prevention, education, treatment, research, law enforcement, interdiction, and illicit drug crop reduction to deal with illegal drug use across the spectrum of human organization. We cannot stop drug use and abuse in America while allowing traffickers to subvert other governments, establish safe-havens in some countries, or overwhelm the capabilities of local law enforcement. . . .

> *"Our nation's domestic challenge is to reduce drug use and its consequences while protecting individual liberties."*

Some people believe that drug use is so deeply embedded in society that we can never hope to decrease it. Others feel that the problem can be solved in short order if draconian measures are adopted. Avoiding extremes, the *1989 National Drug Control Strategy* rejects both of these views. We can reduce drug use without compromising American ideals if we maintain adequate resolve. . . .

An Enduring Challenge

Drug abuse has plagued America for more than a century. To turn that negative experience around will require perseverance and vigilance. Our nation can contain and decrease the damage wrought by drug abuse and its consequences. But we will have to apply ourselves with a resolve marked by continuing education for our citizens, the determination to resist criminals who traffic in illegal drugs, and the patience and compassion to treat individuals caught in the grip of illegal drugs.

The metaphor of a "war on drugs" is misleading. Wars are expected to end. Addressing drug abuse is a continuous challenge; the moment we believe ourselves to be victorious and free to relax our resolve, drug abuse will rise again. Furthermore, the United States does not wage war on its citizens, many of whom are the victims of drug abuse. These individuals must be helped, not defeated. It is the suppliers of illegal drugs, both foreign and domestic, who must be thwarted.

A more appropriate analogy for the drug problem is cancer. Dealing with cancer is a long-term proposition. It requires the mobilization of support mechanisms—human, medical, educational, and societal, among others—to check its spread, deal with its consequences, and improve the prognosis. Resistance to its spread is necessary, but so is patience, compassion, and the will to carry on against its inroads. Pain must be managed while the root cause is attacked. The road to recovery is long and complex.

Decreasing illegal drug use in America is a difficult task. . . . The duty of the federal government is to help communities resist drug abuse and overcome its consequences. Ultimately, each American must make his or her own decision about whether to begin or stop using illegal drugs and how to enable communities to overcome the impact of drug abuse.

Government Leadership and Community Efforts Can Win the War on Drugs

by Robert B. Charles

About the author: *Robert B. Charles served as chief of staff and chief counsel to the House Subcommittee on National Security, International Affairs, and Criminal Justice in 1997.*

In America, you increasingly hear the tone of defeatism when the topic of drugs works its way into public conversation (as it will continue to do for some time). Common are phrases like "the drug war is unwinnable" and "what's wrong with legalization, anyway." Pundits and legalization advocates routinely (and somewhat gleefully) oscillate between two extremes, calling the drug war insoluble and treating drugs as no problem at all. The truth, on both counts, is quite different. I grew up in Maine, and have seen the impact of drugs there from Lewiston and Portland to Winthrop and Readfield. However, after two years in Washington, as chief of staff and chief counsel to a congressional committee charged with oversight of the nation's drug war, I have gotten a brutal education, much of it disturbing, some of it hopeful, almost all of it previously unknown (at least to me).

First, the threat posed by widening drug abuse among teens, powerful international drug cartels, drug-related violent crime and the increasing impact of drugs on our nation's character is plainly enormous. On the other hand, it must be acknowledged that the resources available to confront this threat, both federally and locally, have hardly been tapped.

These two facts, in early 1995, spurred the new Republican Congress to initiate what I sincerely believe are significant steps toward reversing the riptide of drug abuse, drug trafficking and violent drug crime. These hopeful steps range from novel drug prevention efforts, such as the Drug Free Communities Act of 1997, to a massive 1996 infusion of funding for law enforcement (including

Reprinted from "Fight to Win the Drug War," by Robert B. Charles, *Portland (Maine) Press Herald*, April 27, 1997.

Byrne Grants, which help finance the Drug Abuse Resistance Education (D.A.R.E.). antidrug program), drug interdiction and international antidrug programs. A little history is worth recounting. Somehow, between 1992 and 1995, we seem to have lost our way as a nation and stumbled. That stumble hurt us, and it hurt our kids. The facts are now a matter of public record.

Recent Drug Policies

In 1992, President George Bush committed $1.5 billion to drug interdiction. In 1993, President Bill Clinton cut $200 million out of that interdiction effort and mothballed U.S. Customs' antidrug aircraft (the sort that found and pursued traffickers from Colombia). Clinton transferred intelligence gathering aircraft out of the Caribbean, rolled back National Guard involvement in antidrug efforts (a vital part of our border and internal program), halved the number of Coast Guard cutters, ship days, flying hours, and personnel dedicated to drug interdiction and left much of the U.S. border (both in the Southwest and in places like Maine) vulnerable.

Sadly, these lost assets did not reappear in the federal budget dedicated to drug prevention or law enforcement. In fact, the president cut his own antidrug policy office from 146 persons down to 25. What is more, he did not feel compelled to speak more than two dozen times on the topic of drugs in more than 2,600 speeches and interviews during 1993 and 1994. Plainly, drugs were not a priority. In 1994, the administration further cut drug interdiction by $18 million; in 1995, it fell by another $15 million. By 1996, President Clinton's strategy had put drug interdiction at a level nearly $100 million below the 1992 level, and source country programs (dedicated to ideas like coca crop eradication and alternative crop production in places like Peru, Bolivia and Colombia) at $123 million below their 1992 levels.

These were discouraging signs even to many who supported the president. We now know that his own chiefs of the FBI, Drug Enforcement Agency and Coast Guard independently (albeit internally) warned that this approach could yield a deadly harvest. They were right.

In 1996, for the third year in a row, 400 tons of cocaine entered our country, roughly 70 percent over our border with Mexico, and the rest along northern and coastal borders from Maine to Puerto Rico. Mexico produced 150 tons of methamphetamine,

> *"The threat posed by widening drug abuse among teens, powerful international drug cartels, drug-related violent crime . . . is plainly enormous."*

a deadly drug ravaging California and working its way eastward. Mexican drug cartels now ship two deadly types of heroin north, and a marijuana that is 25 times more potent than what Maine saw in the 1970s.

As a nation, we are under siege. Other statistics are more poignant. At home, we lose more than 10,000 children annually to drugs and drug-related crime, all avoidable. If any other foe inflicted human havoc on that scale, especially on our vulnerable and precious children, we would respond with fury. But not, it seems, if the foe is a drug cartel or trafficker, pusher or legalizer.

From 1994 to 1997, we have witnessed a 200 percent increase in drug use by the nation's children ages 8 to 17. At the same time, the price of dangerous drugs has fallen dramatically, availability has risen and the street purity of cocaine, heroin and marijuana is greater.

Children Enticed

Young teens and younger children are being drawn into the vortex of addiction; I recently saw LSD (whose popularity is increasing in many areas) marketed with the Lion King and Mickey Mouse on it. I ask parents: Do you think that these traffickers are target-marketing "The Lion King" to 16-year-olds? If so, think again. (Sadly, only about 25 percent of parents talk to their kids about drugs.)

In 1997, for the fourth year in a row, the Drug Abuse Warning Network, which collects emergency room data from across the nation, reported record-level emergency room admissions for cocaine, heroin, methamphetamines, and THC or marijuana, many involving youngsters. In 1995, overall drug-related emergency room episodes jumped 12 percent. Cocaine-related episodes rose 21 percent. And heroin-related episodes skyrocketed 27 percent

THC or marijuana related emergencies, as a result of higher purities and the lacing of marijuana with PCP, were up 32 percent. And methamphetamine emergencies were up

> *"We lose more than 10,000 children annually to drugs and drug-related crime, all avoidable."*

35 percent. Supply and purity are so high, and prices so low, that kids can buy or have pushed on them drugs that were unaffordable and unavailable 10 years ago. And these drugs are destroying young lives in record numbers.

In 1994, there were 750,000 more teenagers using drugs than in 1992, a reversal of the 1981 to 1992 downward trend. Even the Justice Department made the point recently that drug-related violent juvenile crime may double by the year 2010 if we do not turn it back now.

Communities Must Rally

So, where is the hope? Dwelling on past mistakes if futile. We must get beyond regret, partisanship, and fear into the light of a reenergized effort to bring communities together in an effort involving both community and federal leadership. We must reclaim our streets, schools, homes, and children—in short, the nation's future. How? . . .

On the domestic side, there is a bold approach. The Drug Free Communities Act of 1997 offered between $50,000 and $100,000 to any community in America that can sustain, for six months, a strong, high-participation, antidrug coalition (including parents, teachers, businesses, law enforcement officers, churches, doctors, policy-makers and others). In this law, which requires the birth and survival of a successful volunteer antidrug effort before federal funds appear, there is both flexibility and accountability. . . .

Added Support Expected

Also on the domestic side, expect congressional efforts to enhance border support, from Operation Sledgehammer off the coast of Maine to more personnel and analysts at DEA and Customs. Perhaps more importantly, crucial state and local law enforcement programs will get added support, such as the New England State Police Information Network or NESPIN, which allows local law enforcement to network nationwide on a secure database when following criminal leads.

That federally funded database—the Regional Information Sharing System (RISS)—has already proved invaluable to law enforcement officers.

On the international side, there is again reason for hope. The new Congress disagreed, in 1995 and 1996, with the deep cuts in drug interdiction, international drug programs, and the president's own office. Congress insisted that the White House dedicate 154 employees (instead of 25) to the drug problem, added new funds for drug prevention, refocused drug treatment on proven techniques, instilled discipline (by statute) in each of the 50 agencies with a role in the drug war, insisted on measurable goals (lacking since 1992), and began the Bipartisan Drug Policy Working Group (attended by congressional Republicans and Democrats, as well as by the administration). These are small but positive steps.

On federal funding, the new Congress in 1996 increased DEA's budget by $172 million, $20 million over the president's request, and added 75 new DEA agents. International programs received $35 million more than in 1995, and the National Guard, Coast Guard, Border Patrol and military support for the drug war (which is growing) all increased.

The truth: We are a long way from success, which I define as a drug-free America. But with 70 percent of all crime in America stemming from substance abuse or drug trafficking (including 80 percent of all domestic violence and most property and violent crime), we must all resolve to forge ahead.

> *"Supply and purity are so high, and prices so low, that kids can buy . . . drugs that were unaffordable and unavailable 10 years ago."*

In Washington, where ice fishing, "mud season," black flies and cheap lobster are things of vacation, we are trying. But elsewhere, where parents care, there remains a deep concern about the values we pass to our kids, not to mention their safety and well-being. It is essential that we not forget the threat that drugs and related crime pose. There is no room for cynicism in this new world, and no time for those who dare to think the drug war is either insoluble or unimportant.

Chapter 1

The great leaders of another war were once described as "breathing in fear and breathing out confidence." That is the mission that awaits us today. To build community antidrug coalitions. Talk with our kids about drugs. Demand more of our leaders, and more of ourselves. We must cast off words like unwinnable, and dig in for the fight. Only if we believe in our children and in their future, will they believe in themselves and in the same drug-free society that we hope for them.

Interdiction and Prevention Efforts Can Win the War on Drugs

by William J. Bennett

About the author: *William J. Bennett was the director of the Office of National Drug Control Policy under President George Bush and is co-chairman of the Partnership for a Drug-Free America.*

In 2001, President George W. Bush announced the nomination of John P. Walters to serve as the director of the Office of National Drug Control Policy. The drug czar is being asked to lead the nation's war on illegal drugs at a time when many are urging surrender.

The forms of surrender are manifold: Buzzwords like "harm reduction" are crowding out clear no-use messages. State initiatives promoting "medical marijuana" are little more than thinly veiled legalization efforts (as underscored by the May 2001 8-0 Supreme Court ruling against medical exceptions). The 2001 film "Traffic" portrayed the war on drugs as a futile effort. In a survey by the Pew Research Center for the People and the Press, 74 percent of Americans believe the war on drugs is a failure.

Drug Control Programs Are Successful

And yet recent history shows that, far from being a failure, drug control programs are among the most successful public policy efforts of the latter half of the 20th century. According to a national drug survey, between 1979 and 1992, the most intense period of antidrug efforts, the rate of illegal drug use dropped by more than half, while marijuana use decreased by two-thirds. Cocaine use dropped by three-fourths between 1985 and 1992.

Why is this record described as a failure? For those who would legalize drugs, all drug control efforts must be painted as disastrous. But for most Americans, frustration with the drug issue stems from the fact that over the past eight

Reprinted from "The Drug War Worked Once; It Can Again," by William J. Bennett, *The Wall Street Journal*, May 15, 2001, by permission of *The Wall Street Journal* and the author. Copyright © 2001, Dow Jones & Company, Inc. All rights reserved.

years we have lost ground.

During the Bill Clinton administration, our nation's drug policy suffered a period of malign neglect. Clinton's two clearest statements about illegal drugs were his infamous statement "I didn't inhale" and his immediate and dramatic cut in the size of the federal antidrug staff. Morale and political leadership were both compromised, and a national cynicism about drug use resulted. Hiring a four-star general [Barry McCaffrey] may have fooled the public and the Washington press corps for a while, but it didn't add up to a meaningful program.

To paraphrase [the playwright] Arthur Miller, attention was not paid, and the problem quickly worsened: Between 1992 and 1999, rates of current drug use—defined as using once a month or more—increased by 15 percent. Rates of marijuana use increased 11 percent. The situation was far worse among our children: Lifetime use of illegal drugs increased by 37 percent among eighth graders and 55 percent among tenth graders. We have reached the point where more than one-quarter of all high school seniors are current users of illegal drugs; indeed, rates of monthly drug use among high school seniors increased 86 percent between 1992 and 1999.

We must re-engage this fight. What we were doing in the 1980s and early 1990s—vigorous law enforcement and interdiction coupled with effective prevention and treatment—worked. It can work again.

Prevention Strategies Work

The most important component of any antidrug strategy is prevention. Children who reach the age of 21 without using illegal drugs are almost certain never to do so. The Partnership for a Drug-Free America has crafted some of the most memorable and effective advertisements in history, encouraging children to turn down illegal drugs. The message that drug use is dangerous and immoral is the essential key to prevention.

In addition, we must continue to develop effective treatment programs. Many criticisms have been leveled at America's lack of treatment capacity, but more troubling is the lack of treatment efficacy. However, 12-step programs (akin to Alcoholics Anonymous) have been shown to be both inexpensive and effective in private sector drug treatment. Hopefully, their success can be extended to public sector treatment as well.

"Drug control programs are among the most successful public policy efforts of the latter half of the 20th century."

Most agree on the necessity of effective treatment and strong prevention efforts. Some people, however, believe that law enforcement should have no role in the process. This is an altogether simplistic model: Demand reduction cannot be effective without supply reduction.

It is true that there will always be a supply of illegal drugs as long as there is a demand. But forceful interdiction can help to increase the price and decrease the purity of drugs available, a critical means of intervening in the lives of addicts, who can only beg, borrow and steal so much to support their habit. Government reports document that recovering addicts are more likely to relapse when faced with cheap, plentiful drugs. Aggressive interdiction efforts, then, are not supply reduction so much as the first step in demand reduction.

Demand Reduction Efforts

Some people will admit that there is a place for law enforcement, but contend we spend too much on this effort, to the detriment of demand reduction. In fact, according to Robert DuPont, who led the nation's antidrug efforts under Presidents Nixon and Ford, there has never been as much federal money spent on prevention education as is being spent today. The United States' total spending on drug-demand reduction far exceeds the amounts spent in the rest of the world combined.

A more pragmatic point: While treatment is often centered at the individual and local levels, interdiction and law enforcement must be federal responsibilities. Given the scope and complexity of drug trafficking, the federal government can and must assume the responsibility for stopping the traffic of drugs across and within our borders. The drug czar's first concerns, then, must be interdiction and law enforcement, if only because they are tasks no other agency can perform as effectively.

> *"What we were doing in the 1980s and early 1990s—vigorous law enforcement and interdiction coupled with effective prevention and treatment—worked."*

I believe that the position of drug czar ought to remain at the Cabinet level, but more important is the president's personal support and commitment to the office. I had that backing, and I expect the new drug czar will enjoy that same support and commitment from Bush. If Walters is to have any success, he must enjoy it.

The past eight years are, once again, illustrative: General Barry McCaffrey never enjoyed that support from then President Clinton. In renewing the drug war, the new drug czar will not be alone. He will be able to draw on the assistance of people—parents, teachers, substance-abuse counselors, clergymen and elected officials—who have continued to fight drug use over the past eight years. These groups are our first lines of defense; without them, the regression since 1992 would have been far worse. Their dedication gives the lie to the gospel of futility.

I look forward to America re-engaging in the war on drugs—and continuing the success that we had between 1980 and 1992.

The War on Drugs Has Been Unsuccessful

by Daniel Spichtinger

About the author: *Daniel Spichtinger works as a journalist and webmaster in Austria.*

Drugs are often, especially in the mass media, portrayed as a threat of enormous proportions. They are held responsible for all sorts of problems like crime, (assumed) moral decay and unemployment, to name only a few. Thus, more and more extreme measures are introduced to win the war on drugs. This essay will not only try to define the somewhat vague term "war on drugs", it will also give the major theories about the true purpose of the war and it will present alternative models of how to deal with the drug problem.

In 1986 Ronald Reagan held a speech in which he officially declared the war on drugs using metaphors of war, illness, crusades and religious righteousness to justify actions against drug users and dealers. According to the psychologist Bruce Alexander such warlike language and violent imagery is part of a possible definition of the war on drugs. When drug users are described as a menace to society, steps to eradicate the "enemy" are met with little resistance from the public. Alexander considers the enhance in police power, which results in legal violence, spying, and an increase in illegal violence to be further characteristics of the war against drugs.

A History of the Drug War

To understand the current situation, it is necessary to go back to the beginning of the twentieth century. The Harrison Narcotics Act of 1914 heavily taxed the opium trade. Much worse, however, was the fact that a clause in the Act allowed law enforcement personnel to arrest physicians who prescribed opiates. This led to the creation of a big black market and many addicts were thus forced to turn to crime to maintain their addiction. The reasons for the Harrison Act were mainly a racist attitude toward immigrants from the Pacific Rim and a

Reprinted, with permission, from "The War on Drugs," by Daniel Spichtinger, 1996, found at www. geocities.com/dspichtinger/mtexts/wod.htm.

moralistic tide which swept through the country and eventually led to the prohibition of most psychoactive drugs and gave control to the police.

However, the background reasons of the ongoing war on drugs are much more complex. Bruce Alexander tries to explain the war by subdividing society in various groups: the drug warriors are the proponents of the war on drugs; the resisters are totally against it; and the neutrals do not care about the problem. For Alexander the drug war is a war between two philosophies of life. The warriors, on the one hand, feel a strong need to enforce societal power and to suppress personal autonomy and are concerned that drug use reduces the compliance with social conventions. The resisters, on the other hand, place individual autonomy well over societal control.

Another possible explanation is offered by conflict theory, which sees the war on drugs as a polarisation of conservative forces against left wing political activists and minority members. The theory basically assumes that the powerful in society selectively criminalize actions of those who are subordinate to them. The enforcement actions of the war on drugs seem indeed to be focused against minorities. According to conflict theory, this is the case because the powerful want to take attention away from underlying factors; the dominant groups want to legislate their lifestyle and culture in others in order to maintain their hegemony. Conservatives admit that what makes drugs a serious problem (for them) is less its medical aspect than its social purpose.

A similar view is offered by a theory called social construction of the drug problems. It assumes that the media's constant reports on the threat of drugs, the evil, crime, death, insanity and the pictures of crack babies create a social perception of a problem when in reality there is none. The immorality of drug use is again and again used as a justification for strict laws. Ethan Nadelmann, a professor at Princeton, points out that drug prohibition has created a permanent underclass of unemployable inner-city youths, whose lives are interwoven with drugs and crime. Thus, if the war on drugs really is a social construction, it is a superbly constructed one.

The Iran Contra Affair

The situation of drug users was worsened during the presidency of George Bush from 1988 to 1992. The Bush era is particularly interesting because much has been found out about his dubious role in the drug war. When Bush won the election in 1988 people said the budget was America's biggest problem; only three percent named drugs. After Bush's media campaign, 40–45 percent said drugs were America's biggest problem. On the one hand, George Bush introduced tougher laws and allocated new funds for law enforcement. Furthermore, the Bush era Supreme Court upheld police power to detain and interrogate travellers resembling drug couriers and to secretly tap conversations. On the other hand his involvement in CIA activities during the Iran Contra affair is more or less proven. During the 1980's the CIA waged a covert war in Central America against the Marxist Sandinista Party. The CIA and the Nicaraguan Contras were involved in drugs-for-guns barter arrangements. This is proven by the fact that—because of guns and drug smuggling—Lt. Col. Oliver North and other White House assistants were banned for life from entering Costa Rica in 1989. Furthermore, General Manuel Noriega, later overthrown by Bush because of his involvement with drug cartels, was on the CIA payroll during the 1970's and 1980's. It is extremely unlikely that George Bush, former head of the CIA and Vice President, knew nothing about all this.

Bush's predecessor Ronald Reagan's drug policy was also not successful. He started a massive eradication program called Operation Delta Nine. Troops and helicopters were used against domestic marijuana growers in all 50 states. Unfortunately, this only served to put the competitors of the Colombian Medellin cartel out of business, and thus secured the market for the cartel. Reagan's wife Nancy's "Just say No" campaign which emphasised the destructiveness of drugs to families and the cost to business was eventually replaced by several new drug education programs. The largest and costliest is D.A.R.E., which stands for Drug Abuse Resistance Education. Developed under direction of former Los Angeles Police chief Daryl Gates, the program is taught by uniformed cops to students from kindergarten to twelfth grade. However, critics claim that the course material, methods of delivery and basic philosophical premise are seriously flawed and point out that the content of D.A.R.E. is not only taught in D.A.R.E. courses but also in other areas like math or spelling.

> *"When drug users are described as a menace to society, steps to eradicate the 'enemy' are met with little resistance from the public."*

They say that better programs exist and that D.A.R.E. might do more harm than good. Another organisation with access to a broad audience is the Partnership for a Drug Free America which continues to censor important drug data and produces a simplistic view of illegal drugs. In addition, the partnership has accepted contributions from legal drug manufactures and therefore only deals with illegal drugs but not with alcohol or tobacco.

America's Prisons

One of the most obvious effects of the war on drugs is the enormous increase in prisoners. Since 1970 the percentage of Americans in prison has tripled. At present, 1.3 million citizens of the United States serve a prison sentence; in other words, five out of 1000 Americans are in jail. Not only does that make the United States the country with the highest percentage of its citizens in correctional facilities, it also forces the government to add 1000 prison beds each week! California, for example, has built 18 new prisons in the last 12 years (five more are planned) but no college in over 27 years. 75% of all inmates in California serve for drug or drug-related crimes. Because the appointment of judges, the feeding, clothing and maintaining of prisoners—not to speak of the actual building of prisons—are big business, many corporations want to keep drugs illegal. Although President Bill Clinton has admitted that "we cannot jail our way out of the problem" his Na-tional Drug Control Strategy, intro-duced in 1994, does not sound much different than that of his predeces-sors, and the emphasis remains on law enforcement. Moreover, the huge profits that can be made ensure that every time a criminal is convicted someone is ready to take his place.

> *"Drug prohibition has created a permanent underclass of unemployable inner-city youths, whose lives are interwoven with drugs and crime."*

Nevertheless, it has to be pointed out that many addiction experts are not in favour of decriminalisation. They think legalising drugs would lead to a sharp rise in use and advocate that the current policy of zero tolerance against drugs should be retained. Because drugs would be cheaper, addicts would buy more of them and would spend more time using them and less time working. Therefore, they would continue to commit crimes to acquire money. These experts conclude that through the increase of addicts that comes with legalisation crime would also in-crease. Many politicians who are in favour of zero tolerance policy agree with this statement and think that drug users deserve the worst of fates. Former Los Angeles police chief Daryl Gates advised the senate that "casual users should be taken out and shot." Furthermore, Newt Gingrich says mandatory executions for convicted drug smugglers would kill so many that it would curb the flow of ille-gal drugs to the United States. People who smuggled large quantities of drugs "wouldn't have ten years of playing games with the system" but should only have one appeal and 18 months to fight their conviction.

This opinion is not shared by the Mayor of Baltimore, Kurt Schmoke. He ar-gues that the violence connected with drugs is caused by the failed national drug strategy which makes the drug trade enormously profitable. He thinks that decriminalisation would greatly reduce violent and property crimes. Schmoke points out that there are 48,000 addicts in Baltimore but only 5,300 treatment slots and sees this as a root cause for many of the city's problems. Moreover, many deaths of addicts result from use of contaminated drugs and could be pre-vented. Consequently, Schmoke thinks that legalisation is a reasonable alterna-tive to the war on drugs. Legalisation could take many forms. The libertarian concept, for example, wants a free market distribution of all drugs, while the proponents of a controlled distribution concept argue that there should be a sys-tem similar to alcohol and tobacco licensing and taxation.

Harm Reduction

Another alternative to the war on drugs is the harm reduction model that is used in the Netherlands, Australia and the UK. It concentrates on the community and individual level and tries to reduce the negative consequences of drug use through, among other things, needle exchange programs. Merseyside, near Liverpool, is the model city of this approach. Here clinics, doctors, pharmacists and the police work together and try to treat the user on an individual basis. Emphasis is on getting many different people involved which gives people the feeling that they are helping to solve a serious problem. The model reduces the conflict between user and community, and results have so far been encouraging. In the Netherlands the goal has been to make marijuana boring through legalising the drug, and since decriminalisation the use of marijuana has steadily declined. Through decriminalisation (or harm reduction) money that was once allocated to enforcement could be budgeted for education and treatment programs.

From all the arguments which were presented the reader will easily realise that the war on drugs has not been successful. Although the laws against drugs have become stricter and stricter and basic civil rights have been diminished, draconian penalties have not reduced the crime and violence connected with drugs, the police have become more brutal, particularly against minorities, and—worst of all—the population has lost faith in the rationality of the government. Everything indicates that the war on drugs cannot be won, and it would be time to consider an alternative drug policy. The real threat is not the misuse of drugs but that the habits of liberty, citizen responsibility and tolerance fall into disuse. In the words of President Eisenhower: "We must guard against the acquisition of unwarranted influence. . . . The potential for disastrous rise of misplaced power exists and will persist."

The War on Drugs Causes More Harm than Good

by Mark Steyn

About the author: *Mark Steyn is a theater critic for the* New Criterion, *a magazine of cultural criticism, and a movie critic for the* Spectator, *a British political affairs magazine.*

The State of New Hampshire doesn't require much from its school districts—a mutually satisfactory arrangement about to be abruptly terminated due to an asinine Supreme Court decision declaring our entire education system unconstitutional.

But I digress. One of the few things the state does require of my small grade school and every other one is that they post signs on the road warning motorists they are now entering a "Drug-Free School Zone."

It irks me. At board meetings, I'm tempted to stand up and demand we replace it with "You Are Now Entering a Latin-Free School Zone"—which at least has the merit of being indisputable. But it seems the best we can hope for from our public education system these days is that our children aren't heroin dealers by the time they've been through it. And instead of being quietly ashamed of this stunted redefinition of education, we flaunt it as a badge of pride, out on the highway, even at a rural north country elementary school. For even kindergartners and first-graders must understand that they, too, are footsoldiers in the "war on drugs." Best of all, like almost all other awards in the American school system, you get it automatically: every educational establishment in the state triumphantly displays the same sign, regardless of whether it's a Drug-Free School Zone or a School-Free Drug Zone.

And that's more or less how the "war on drugs" goes for grown-ups, too. South of the Mexican border, they're nailing up their 1999 "Proud to Be Recognized As a Full Partner in the War on Drugs" signs, recently shipped out by the U.S. government. It doesn't actually matter whether the Mexican authorities are cracking down on their drug barons or whether their so-called "drug czar" and

Excerpted from "Call Off the Drug War: America Blames Everyone but Itself for Its Habits," by Mark Steyn, *The American Spectator*, April 1999. Copyright © 1999 The American Spectator. Reprinted with permission.

half the cops are on the take; Washington still "recertifies" them, because not to do so could send "the wrong signal."

I have some sympathy for these harassed Latins. What's known here as "America's drug problem" might more properly be described as the rest of the world's America problem. Americans like drugs. Americans consume drugs in large quantities. And yet, because as a nation Americans are still sufficiently hypocritical to be unwilling formally to acknowledge their appetites, the burden of servicing this huge market has shifted inexorably to the dusty ramshackle statelets in America's backyard. It may well be true that most Mexican police and most Colombian politicians are corrupt, but why wouldn't they be? . . .

Government Hypocrisy

[The war on drugs has taken an interesting turn.] In 1996, California and Arizona passed propositions decriminalizing marijuana or mandating it "for medicinal purposes." Let us stipulate that, if you believe the latter, you've been inhaling too long: No doubt marijuana has no more medicinal properties than, say, butterscotch pudding. Let us stipulate, also, that most proponents of "medicinal marijuana" are those whose principal enthusiasm for the drug is strictly non-medicinal. But, even so, there's something very curious about the vigor with which this administration—led by a president who smirkingly told MTV viewers that, given another chance, he'd inhale—has been determined to reverse the voters' decision and harass any doctors who support it. Nothing, it seems, can deflect the federal government from its "war." It's an interesting case study in addiction: Like some crack-frazzled zombie, the government staggers on blindly, unable to be weaned from its self-destructive and sociopathic course.

In America there are two problems: drugs, and the "war on drugs"; and the "war" is the bigger one. Yes, drugs are a danger to society—though, on balance, they're probably not as big a threat as America's Number One addiction, food. The fact that over 50 percent of the population is now classified as overweight has far more serious consequences for society than drugs do. Yet no one suggests driving hamburgers underground, forcing junk-food junkies into the arms of back-alley "Mac" dealers. ("Yeah, he, like, told me it was 100 percent pure ground Argentine, but, like, it turned out to be a lethal cocktail of dog turd and English beef. That's real bad s—t, man—'specially the English stuff.")

> *"What's known here as 'America's drug problem' might more properly be described as the rest of the world's America problem."*

Or take gay sex. Given HIV rates of 50–60 percent among homosexuals in New York and San Francisco, you could easily make the case that gay sex is harmful and should be banned. Nobody does, though. Au contraire, vast resources are devoted to finding ways of making it less harmful, from protease inhibitors to the race to invent the concrete condom. The government reckons that, since most guys who wanna do it are gonna do it anyway, better to figure out ways to make it safer.

Not so with drugs, where the "war" floats free of budgetary constraints and there's enough government largesse to swill around the DEA, ATF, FBI, and at least 50 other agencies. When former Vice President Gore suggested amalgamating these warring, inefficient, acronymic agencies into one slimmed-down ultra-efficient DEATFBI, the president ruled against it on the grounds that it would send (all together now) the "wrong signal": having lots of agencies, no matter how useless, sends the right signal. So, across the country, undercover DEA agents are staking out undercover FBI agents who are selling drugs to undercover DEA agents who are staking out undercover ATF agents.

Mixed Signals

Still, the signals the present system's sending are, to say the least, mixed. In 1996, it was revealed that, as part of their infiltration of one Latin American drug cartel, federal agents had successfully smuggled millions of dollars' worth of cocaine onto the streets of America's cities. At that level, it's hard to see the difference between successful infiltration and full-scale participation. But given their adeptness at managing the drug trade, these guys might at least manage it on behalf of the U.S. Treasury rather than some pock-marked bozos from Colombia.

N. Scott Stevens, my near-neighbor in New Hampshire and the head of

> *"In America there are two problems: drugs, and the 'war on drugs'; and the 'war' is the bigger one."*

the White Mountain Militia, thinks there's a lot of this going on. He doesn't do drugs, but he doesn't think the federal government has the right to legislate what you grow in your yard and, anyway, to criminalize it only corrupts the feds. "The amount of drugs in this country, there's no way they're all coming in on Piper Cubs. Those guys have got foreign bank accounts, they're running three or four cars, they're wearing silk suits." Funnily enough, federal agencies never seem to notice those sorts of things. In 1995, over the river in tiny Cavendish, Vermont, a team of seven fully-armed DEA agents in bullet-proof vests swooped down out of nowhere at 3 a.m. on the home of a small-town lawyer, Will Hunter, and then announced to the world that "it is clear" he'd been laundering drug money: no "allegedlys," no "the investigation is ongoing," just "it is clear." They took three years to indict him for anything, and eventually settled for a single count of mail fraud. Hunter was making about $20,000 a year and routinely took payment in cheese and maple syrup. Possibly, this was just a brilliant facade, albeit one he kept up 24 hours a day, 365 days a year. But I went round to his cramped little Cape, with one bath, with the family's pet turtle in it, and all I can say is, if he's laundering anything other than maple syrup, he's doing it far more discreetly than, say, Aldrich Ames, the CIA traitor whose brand-new Merc and half-million dollar home paid for in cash apparently never aroused the suspicion of his colleagues.

Snitch

But, with undercover federal agents now commanding such a huge slice of the drug business, the cannier dealers have begun to figure out that, instead of selling drugs in such a crowded and competitive market, it's easier and more profitable to sell drug suspects to the DEA. A Bolivian on the lam from his own cops, and wanted in Argentina for every scam going, washed up in Washington and, after a fruitless attempt to sell his wife's heart, lungs, and kidneys as she lay in a coma, finally hit the federal gravy train. He called a DEA office in Southern California and claimed that, if they could get the charges in Bolivia and Argentina dropped and fix U.S. residency for him, he could deliver them "Chama," the East Coast distributor for a huge South American cartel. Not only did they do that, they paid him $30,000 plus expenses and several flights to California into the bargain. The phone call to a West Coast office was a stroke of genius: He knew that the Californians would be terrified of losing the case to East Coast agents and so would keep it a secret. The only problem was there was no "Chama," so instead he gave them the name of a guy he knew, a parking lot attendant who worked 60 hours a week for minimum wage. The guy punches a time clock, so his records can be verified, but so what? It never occurred to the DEA to wonder why the East Coast King of Cocaine is parking cars 60 hours a week and living in a one-room apartment. Instead, they call him up at home and try to entrap him. This is their end of the conversation:

"Yeah, what I'm trying to do is—since it's a matter which is quite serious—big—and from the other things that I've seen like this, when we can't be playing with, with unclear words and . . . that's why what I, what you did, and I asked you if you'd spoken with him, because I know that he has the financial capacity and after all he's, he's a partner of, of, of, and, and in the end anything will yield a profit if we're hanging on to a big stick that's on a big branch and, and we won't have any problems. Right?"

The minimum-wage car-parker, being Bolivian and not speaking much English but familiar with America's many telephone salesmen, replies: "Of course."

> *"Dealers have begun to figure out that . . . it's easier and more profitable to sell drug suspects to the DEA."*

On the strength of this, the DEA launched an eight-month investigation costing hundreds of thousands of dollars. With most cases, the informant has to wheedle out a small sample of cocaine from the trafficker to prove to the feds that he's really in the business. No sample was forthcoming from the Bolivian car-parker, mainly because he wasn't a drug dealer, but, even if he'd wanted to be, he didn't know anyone who'd sell him any drugs and he didn't have any money to pay for them. But the beauty of this scam was that, according to DEA experts, true Class One dealers never give samples. Therefore, the fact that no cocaine was forthcoming, that there was no cocaine in sight, and that there was no evidence that the poor chump had ever been in the same room as any cocaine was only further proof that the guy must be a real Mister Big.

Excessive Regulation

Which goes to show that no matter how crack addles the brain, it's nothing to what investigating crack does to it. We've learned to live with the remorseless corruption of the "war," but, even so, out in California, the government's pursuit of Peter McWilliams breaks new ground. McWilliams hit the jackpot: he's got AIDS and cancer. But because, like a majority of his fellow Californians, he believes in the right to "medicinal marijuana," he's sitting in jail, facing a ten-year sentence, while prominent supporters of his are staked out by various Federal agencies on apparently limitless budgets. No surprise there. Since 1980, the budget for the "war" has increased by over 1000 percent. Even if he'd been laundering drug money, the raid on that country lawyer in Vermont cost far more than he could ever possibly have laundered.

And all of this is completely unnecessary. If drugs were made legally available in government drugstores, the price would decline, enabling the government to make a tidy profit and addicts to cut down on their property theft. You'd get rid of drug crime, drug murder, drug informers, drug cartels—and all those drug agencies. And that's why it'll never happen. Almost

> *"No matter how crack addles the brain, it's nothing to what investigating crack does to it."*

every drug agent could be reassigned to the new departments of the FDA necessary to regulate federal drugstores, supervise the mandatory labeling of every spliff, etc. But I can appreciate that that probably doesn't have the glamour of swooping down in your chopper at dawn and leaping out, guns a-blazing. When I asked Agent Bradley, DEA agent-in-charge for Vermont, why he didn't just drop by at Will Hunter's place at nine in the morning, he sighed, "Mark, that's not the way we do things."

Pity. Because all the evidence shows that no one can regulate you into the ground like the U.S. government: Look at those smokers huddled on sidewalks; look at those tobacco companies, constantly fending off one government shakedown after another, no matter how furiously they spread their dough around Washington; look at the poor gun manufacturers, contemplating the same future. And then look at the Medellin and Cali boys in Colombia snorting all the way to the bank. The "drug war" is a civil war: The problem is American appetites—and there are different ways to manage those. Speaking up for Peter McWilliams, legalization advocate Richard Cowan put it this way:

"Everyone wants to talk about what marijuana does, but no one ever wants to look at what marijuana prohibition does. Marijuana never kicks down your door in the middle of the night. Marijuana never locks up sick and dying people, does not suppress medical research, does not peek in bedroom windows. Even if one takes every reefer madness allegation of the prohibitionists at face value, marijuana prohibition has done far more harm to far more people than marijuana ever could."

The War on Drugs Infringes on Civil Liberties

by Mani Foroohar

About the author: *Mani Foroohar is a student at the University of California, Los Angeles, and a contributing editor to the* Daily Bruin, *the campus newspaper.*

Everyone knows the parable of the emperor with no clothes. The significance of a child being the one to point out the emperor's nudity, as opposed to a sermonizing preacher or self-righteous intellectual, is simple to understand. Neither morality nor logic was responsible for stripping the emperor's veil of falsehood. All it took was the truth.

One can't help but think of this when considering Gary Johnson, the Republican governor of New Mexico, who, despite pressure from power brokers at the top of his own party, has proclaimed that the emperor that is this country's war on drugs is not only naked to the world, but that its body is festering with the sores of moral decay and corruption. In the governor's own words, "The drug problem is getting worse. It's not getting better. . . . It needs to get talked about, and one of the things that's going to get talked about is decriminalization."

He continues: "What I'm trying to do here is launch discussion. . . . I think it is the number one problem facing this country today. . . . We really need to put all options on the table."

Not wishing to make a statement without providing viable ideas to support it, Johnson said that changing laws regarding the possession of marijuana would be a logical "first step" since pot is "probably the least dangerous of the identified narcotic drugs that we have."

The Failed War on Drugs

Johnson is not simply grandstanding, as the facts of the situation point out clearly. Despite massive expenditures, the simple fact is that the war on drugs is a total failure. There is more, not less, drug-related violent crime in the United States today than 30 years ago. Far from protecting citizens, the war has

Reprinted, with permission, from "War on Drugs in U.S. Has Backfired," by Mani Foroohar, *Daily Bruin*, February 25, 2000.

spurred unwarranted searches, asset forfeitures and the imprisonment of literally millions of stable and productive Americans.

Of course, many people have closed their eyes to the truth about the drug war for so long that they can't help but respond negatively to Johnson's common-sense approach. Given how many billions of dollars have been thrown into advertisements that criminalize all drug use without making any distinctions, it is no wonder that many people have trouble divorcing themselves from the illusion of righteousness. This is not a reflection on these people, of course, but a testament to the magnitude of the propaganda machine that has been let loose upon them.

Civil Asset Forfeiture Laws

But no amount of propaganda can make a lie true, and examining the truth of just one tool of the war on drugs is sufficient to illustrate that it is not such a noble crusade. Civil asset forfeiture statutes allow law enforcement agencies to seize money and property without convicting, indicting or arresting the owners for any crime. Indeed, property can be seized even if the owners have been acquitted. Eighty percent of people who have property forfeited are not charged with a crime. Police are allowed to seize any assets that they claim to be involved with illicit drugs.

Civil asset forfeiture is based on the concept that property that is allegedly connected to a crime is itself incriminating, and can be seized and tried in civil court. To challenge the forfeiture, persons who have their property taken must pay a bond of 10 percent of the value of their seized assets. Owners must prove by a "preponderance of the evidence" that their property is innocent of the charges, constituting a complete reversal of the "innocent until proven guilty" principle that our justice system is based upon.

Many people, regardless of their innocence, cannot or do not pursue the expensive, lengthy and unpromising litigation process required to regain their forfeited property. The few who win back their property are not allowed to recover their legal fees. Financial assets are returned without interest. Nor can property owners recover money for the damage caused to their property by the government's actions or negligence.

> *"This country's war on drugs is not only naked to the world, but . . . its body is festering with the sores of moral decay."*

Unquestionably, this concept is in direct opposition to the supposedly inalienable rights guaranteed by the Constitution. Undeniably, it is a violation of the basic principles of human dignity used to formulate the Constitution. Irrefutably, it provides an almost irresistible temptation for police abuse.

And this is one of the mildest forms of enforcement in the hands of the drug warriors. In light of such bleak evidence, it is clear that the drug war has created no winners, but an abundance of losers. The biggest losers are the American citizens, who have seen their cherished rights discarded and continue to suffer decaying schools, nonexistent or inadequate health care, and crumbling infrastructure in poor and rural areas. And still, billions of dollars are poured into a campaign that is nothing more than a ponderous artifact with no place in a free society. The drug war failed a long time ago, and it's time to let it die. That is the naked truth.

The War on Drugs Harms America's Children

by Adam J. Smith and Karynn M. Fish

About the authors: *Adam J. Smith and Karynn M. Fish work as the Associate Director and Program Director, respectively, for the Drug Reform Coordination Network, a national organization dedicated to improving current drug policies.*

When President George W. Bush revealed his drug war plan, which would pull another $2.7 billion from federal coffers to end the illegal narcotics trade, his speech was all about the children. "The job of protecting our children falls to us," he pontificated, calling drugs "the enemies of innocence and hope and ambition."

In 2000 the federal government will spend more than $18 billion to, in Drug Czar Barry McCaffrey's words, "protect the lives of 68 million American children." Two-thirds of that money will be spent on interdiction and enforcement, an effort that McCaffrey says is aimed at "keeping drugs out of the hands of young people." State and local governments are expected to spend twice that much.

But is the drug war really protecting our children? Are our tax dollars, our booming prison industry, our international military aid really keeping illicit drugs away from our kids? The evidence suggests that far from keeping kids safe, drug prohibition actually gives kids more access to drugs, and that the drug war makes their world more dangerous in numerous other ways.

Easy Availability

Marijuana is unquestionably the most commonly used illicit substance in America. There were more than 800,000 marijuana arrests in 1999, 85 percent for simple possession. Enforcement of marijuana laws accounts for the largest proportion of domestic drug war spending—McCaffrey has repeatedly touted "a 12 year-old smoking a joint" as "the most dangerous drug in America."

Yet the 1999 University of Michigan's "Monitoring the Future" survey of 8th, 10th and 12th graders indicates that despite our best efforts at enforcement, nearly 80 percent of 10th graders and nearly 90 percent of 12th graders rate

Excerpted from "How the Drug War Harms, Not Helps, Our Kids," by Adam J. Smith and Karynn M. Fish, *SpeakOut.com*, October 16, 2000. Reprinted by permission of the authors.

marijuana as "fairly easy" or "very easy" to obtain. Those numbers are up slightly since 1992, the first year for which such data exists. As for other illicit drugs, in 1999 cocaine was "easily" available to 25 percent of 8th graders, methamphetamine was "easily" available to 41 percent of 10th graders, and LSD was "easily" available to 45 percent of high school seniors.

Critics of current U.S. drug policy argue that a system of legal, regulated distribution of currently illicit drugs would place these markets under the control of responsible society. But McCaffrey has ridiculed the idea, telling the House Government Reform criminal justice panel on June 16, 1999 that, "American parents clearly don't want children to use a fake ID at the corner store to buy heroin."

The irony, of course, is that under prohibition there are no enforceable age restrictions on the purchase of illegal drugs. The corner store that sells alcohol might lose its state license if it sells booze to minors. But out on the corner itself, no one gets carded.

A survey conducted in 1998 by the Center on Addiction and Substance Abuse, a non-profit organization under the direction of former Secretary of Health, Education and Welfare Joseph Califano, underscores this point. The survey asked 9th through 12th graders which was easiest for them to buy: cigarettes, beer or marijuana. While each age group listed cigarettes as easiest, twice as many 9th graders and a remarkable four times as many 12th graders listed marijuana as easier to buy than beer.

Failure of Prohibition

History shows that we should not be surprised by these statistics. While alcohol prohibition was adopted under the banner of protecting children in 1920, its utter failure in that regard was noted most vividly by those on the front lines. In 1925, Salvation Army Colonel William L. Barker told the *St. Cloud (Minnesota) Press*, "Prohibition has diverted the energies of the Salvation Army from the drunkard in the gutter to the boys and girls in their teens. The work of the Army has completely changed in the past five years . . . Prohibition has so materially affected society that we have girls in our rescue homes who are 14 and 15 years old, while 10 years ago the youngest was in the early twenties." Protecting children, in fact, later became a rallying cry for prohibition's repeal.

> *"Drug prohibition actually gives kids more access to drugs, and . . . the drug war makes their world more dangerous in numerous other ways."*

In addition to being widely available, the drugs being distributed by the underground market today are both more pure and less expensive than ever before. According to the United Nations Office for Drug Control and Crime Prevention, *Global Illicit Drug Trends 1999*, "Over the past decade, inflation-adjusted prices in Western Europe fell by 45 percent for cocaine and 60 percent for heroin. Comparative falls in the United States were about 50 percent for cocaine and 70 percent for heroin."

That same report indicates that in the US, the purity of heroin on the streets has skyrocketed from around 6 percent in 1987 to an average purity of around 37 percent, with some street heroin testing out at 60 percent by 1997.

The dangers to children of such purity levels are twofold. First and most obvious is the increased risk of overdose at such levels, especially given wide fluctuations in purity between one dose and the next. Less obvious, but more pernicious is the ease of entrée into heroin use that such potency provides to young people. At 6 percent purity, injection was the only viable mode of administration. At current levels, however, the drug can be snorted or even smoked, making it more accessible to novice users who would otherwise have shied away. Snorting or smoking heroin, of course, can also be addictive and is likely to lead to IV use in people who do become dependent. . . .

Drug Education

In spite of our efforts to keep kids abstinent, the Monitoring the Future Survey has found that since 1987, between 40 and 60 percent of high school seniors admit that they've tried an illegal drug at least once. In 1999, the figure was 54 percent.

It would be reasonable, then, to assume that some significant portion of our school-based drug education might be directed at the 50 percent of our kids who have chosen not to "just say no." This would put drug education in line with sex education curricula, which, while urging abstinence, offers

"Under prohibition there are no enforceable age restrictions on the purchase of illegal drugs."

students factual information about sexually transmitted diseases and birth control to minimize the dangers of saying yes. But Congress insists that federal monies earmarked for drug education be limited to abstinence-only programs. Kids are told that drugs are dangerous, but they are not told that some drugs, and some drug-taking behaviors, are more dangerous than others, and why. Even though such information could make the difference between life and death.

Joel Brown, director of the Center for Educational Research and Development and lead author of "In their Own Voices," one of the largest and most comprehensive studies to focus on school-based drug education in the United States, says that our zero-tolerance approach not only leaves kids in the dark, but also weakens the impact of legitimate health warnings by discrediting the messenger.

"Our research, along with numerous other studies, shows that young people experience a significant emotional disturbance when their educational experience doesn't match their real life experience in regards to drugs," he says.

The consequences can be far reaching. "The challenges they face are much more complex than just being able to say no to drugs," says Brown. "Eventually they must learn to be responsible decision makers with regards to prescription drugs, alcohol, tobacco and other drugs. So the information they receive is not only insufficient, it ill prepares them for the challenging and complex drug decisions that they will face over their lives.". . .

The Allure of Easy Money

Along with the dangers of drugs themselves, the drug markets fueled by prohibition add yet another temptation—the siren song of easy money. During the first half of the century, prohibition-era gangsters like Al Capone captured the imagination of a nation. Today, drug prohibition has brought us "gangstas." Young and often from impoverished backgrounds, their relative wealth and power, ephemeral as it may be, beckons strongly to young people with risk-taking personalities and entrepreneurial spirits.

As Mike Gray, author of the book *Drug Crazy: How We Got Into This Mess and How We Can Get Out,* notes, "Unfortunately, the young people we're sending up the river are the very ones who hold the keys to the future—the risk-takers, the entrepreneurs, the organizers who know how to compete in a marketplace that would leave the average businessman gasping for air."

An item in the *Miami Herald* dated July 30, 1998, illustrates the potency of the "culture of prohibition" on even the very young. According to the *Herald*, 12 elementary school children in Pompano Beach, Florida came to the attention of local police when they were found playing "drug dealer," handing out baggies of pretend drugs to each other in exchange for play money.

"You expect these little guys to be playing police or firemen but not dope dealer," sheriff's Lt. James Chinn told the Herald. "This hit me right in the face and ruined my day. This is what they see every day."

Zero Tolerance

Given our insistence on prohibition as the one and only acceptable drug control strategy, government response to kids and the drug trade has been predictable, if ineffective. Harsher laws and a growing willingness to charge, sentence and incarcerate minors as adults have cast a wider and wider net of criminalization around youth culture and behaviors. Rarely, if ever, do policymakers address the larger issue of why drug markets are so out of control that "the land of the free" has become the world's leading incarcerator of young people.

According to research by the Justice Policy Institute, between 1985 and 1997, the number of children under 18 incarcerated in adult prisons for drug crimes climbed by more than 1400 percent. Children incarcerated with adults are far more likely to re-offend, to be assaulted, to be raped and to commit suicide than are minors sentenced to juvenile facilities.

Meanwhile, zero tolerance policies and aggressive drug detection practices by police and school officials have made even "good" kids the object of suspicion, and the target of punitive and exclusionary measures.

Anecdotal evidence of zero-tolerance mania abounds, from the would-be valedictorian from Gulf Shores, Alabama who was expelled after a random drug dog search of the school parking lot turned up a tiny amount of unidentified plant matter on the floor of her parents' car; to the Dayton, Ohio 8th grader suspended after she passed a friend a Midol on the school bus for relief of menstrual cramps; to

> *"The drugs being distributed by the underground market today are both more pure and less expensive than ever before."*

a six year-old in Colorado Springs suspended for sharing a lemon drop with a playmate with the admonition that it would make his friend "strong."

Suspension and expulsion, disciplinary actions once reserved as a means to dispose of the most destructive and disruptive of students, are now commonly invoked as the result of intrusive searches designed to unearth drugs even when no obvious evidence of drug taking or selling exists. . . .

Overflowing Prison Populations

Our relentless and punitive prosecution of the drug war against adults, and the subsequent explosion in our prison population, has had dire consequences for children as well. Of the more than 2 million Americans behind bars, at least 450,000 are there for non-violent drug offenses. Many of these prisoners are parents. Nora Callahan, director of the November Coalition, a non-profit organization of drug war prisoners and their families, says there are over one million "drug war orphans" in America. These children, with one or both parents serving time, are more than five times as likely as other kids to end up in prison themselves.

"Many of these kids never get to see their parents, who are often sent to facilities hundreds or even thousands of miles from home," said Callahan. "If they do see them, it's in the context of a prison visit, which can itself be traumatizing. Many are unlikely to be reunited with mom or dad until well into their own adult years, if ever. Whatever one might think about the drug war, about prohibition, even about non-violent drug offenders, the fact is that we are destroying the lives of an inordinate number of children who themselves have done nothing wrong. And, very likely, we are breeding the next generation of inmates."

Casualties of the Drug War

We teach our children that drugs kill, but the drug war exacts its own casualties as well. On the streets of our cities and towns, a perpetual state of war between the police and an ever-present enemy, a war in which anyone—and thus everyone—can be a suspect, leaves many children caught, literally, in the crossfire.

In 1998, 18 year-old high school student Esequiel Hernandez was shot and killed by camouflaged US marines on an anti-narcotics surveillance mission as he herded his family's goats in Redfern, Texas, near the Mexican border. In 1999 in North Carolina, a 15-year-old boy was shot and injured by police when a house he and five other teens had gathered at to play video games was the target of a raid. In 2000, 11-year-old Alberto Sepulveda was accidentally shot in the back and killed by police as they raided his parents' Modesto, California home to enforce a drug warrant.

These are just a few of the hundreds of young casualties of drug war violence. Over the past several years, teens pressured to act as police informants have been brutalized and murdered by drug dealers, others have been killed in the crossfire of drug disputes, and hundreds have died needlessly of overdose because the people they were with were afraid to seek medical assistance for fear of arrest.

The drug war, now in its eighth decade, is a lot of things to a lot of people. To government agencies involved in carrying out its dictates, it is a source of funding. To corporations in the prison, defense, drug testing and other industries, it is a profit center. To politicians, eager to exploit issues for votes, it is an easy rhetorical hook. And to millions of Americans concerned about substance abuse, it is a noble if flawed response to a seemingly intractable problem. What the drug war is not, as indicated by the rising purity and falling prices of illicit drugs, and their pervasiveness in every city, county and town in America, is an effective drug control strategy.

Everyone, on all sides of the drug policy debate, agrees that children should not use recreational drugs. But in our zeal to protect them by passing more laws and building more prisons in response to every new drug scare or every election cycle, we seem to have missed the larger point. That is that prohibition has both deepened and multiplied the very dangers it seeks to abate. Perhaps it is time to re-examine our course. Perhaps it is time that the welfare of our children, rather than our natural but unrealistic urge to banish that which we fear, takes precedence in our policymaking.

The War on Inner-City Drug Traffickers Is Ineffective

by Glenn C. Loury

About the author: *Glenn C. Loury is a professor of economics and the director of the Institute on Race and Social Division at Boston University.*

As everyone knows, America's eternal war on drugs has inflicted collateral damage of immense proportions on black males. Over the last decade, the prison population has exploded with mostly young, non-white, inner-city males caught in the drug trade. In 1992 alone, two-thirds of those admitted to state prisons for drug offenses were black. And the number of black males held in prisons, as a proportion of the adult population, nearly doubled from 3.5 percent in 1985 to 6.7 percent in 1994. (The corresponding number for whites in 1994 was only 0.9 percent.)

Predictably, some academics and civil rights advocates have decried this trend. In his book *Malign Neglect: Race, Crime and Punishment in America*, Michael Tonry, a criminologist at the University of Minnesota, offers a wealth of data to show that the war on drugs caused arrests to rise more rapidly among blacks than whites during the late 1980s. He concludes that the national drug policy is immoral, precisely because of its racially disparate effects. Similarly, some civil libertarians have denounced the mandatory minimum sentences for federal drug offenses because they single out for harsher treatment those (mostly blacks) who traffic in crack cocaine. Possessing as little as five grams (about $500 worth) of crack carries a five-year mandatory minimum sentence, while it takes 100 times as much cocaine to trigger the same automatic sentence.

Where the Drugs Are

Although superficially appealing, these charges of racial discrimination are ultimately unpersuasive. There is nothing necessarily pernicious about a war on

From "Getting a Fix," by Glenn C. Loury, *The New Republic*, June 30, 1997. Copyright © 1997 by The New Republic, Inc. Reprinted by permission of *The New Republic*.

drugs that hits inner-city traffickers hardest. If one is to fight the drug trade, one must go where the action is, and the action is often in black neighborhoods. Economic logic and accidents of history conspire to make low-income, inner-city neighborhoods ideal locations for drug peddlers. A clandestine commerce can flourish with relative impunity in disorganized communities with abandoned property, a substantial population of transients and easy access to major highways. (Street prostitution is also rampant in these areas and, like drug peddling, quite rare in upper-middle-class suburbs.) And because buyers and sellers cannot openly advertise their locations, they must make an educated guess. So once an area acquires the reputation of being a good place to "score," it is likely to remain one.

> *"The number of black males held in prisons . . . nearly doubled from 3.5 percent in 1985 to 6.7 percent in 1994."*

This makes life hell for law-abiding folks, largely poor and black, who are struggling to raise their children in these neighborhoods. Which is why, as Randall Kennedy of Harvard Law School argues in his book *Race, Crime and the Law*, a policy targeted at retail drug traffickers can, despite its impact on black incarceration rates, also provide disproportionate benefits to black communities. Nothing is more certain to signal that the forces of lawlessness and disorder have won out over those of decency and security than the flourishing of an open-air drug market on neighborhood streets.

There is also nothing necessarily wrong with the more severe treatment of crack in sentencing laws. Crack cocaine is a highly addictive, severely debilitating drug that has wreaked havoc on inner-city communities across the country. The crack trade, a lucrative and deadly business in ghetto America, brings with it an alarming level of violence, with profoundly deleterious consequences for residents of these communities.

Kinks in the System

No, the simple fact of a racially disparate incidence of punishment should not foreclose an otherwise effective law enforcement strategy that is color-blind on its face. But is the current strategy really working? This is a critical question because, while disparate racial results are not disqualifying per se, they are nevertheless undesirable. Locking up an ever larger proportion of the adult male residents of inner-city neighborhoods constitutes a cost to society, and this cost must be placed alongside the benefits of a policy to determine its desirability.

Accumulating evidence demonstrates that the punitive anti-drug crusade of the last decade is, in fact, not producing benefits commensurate with its substantial costs. Indeed, the price of illegal drugs is falling, not rising—and drugs are still available on street corners and in alleyways. Moreover, despite the disparate treatment of crack in federal and some state laws (California's, for example), recent research by Jonathan Caulkins of Carnegie Mellon University has shown that the street prices of crack and powder cocaine are about the same. If so, then the strenuous efforts to target trafficking in crack have had little effect on its supply and thus overall distribution.

Given such evidence, Peter Reuter, a leading drug policy analyst at the University of Maryland's School of Public Affairs, recently argued that our drug policy is now too punitive. In a speech delivered in February 1997 to the National Institute of Justice titled "Can We Make Prohibition Work Better?" Reuter contended that we could "mitigate the harshness of our [drug] policies with little risk of seeing an expansion of drug use and related problems." If, indeed, we can do so, there is a strong argument that we should. Such a mitigation would allow federal and state judges the flexibility to give shorter sentences to retail drug sellers; police to de-emphasize the arrest of users for simple possession; and states to shift at least some resources from punishment into prevention and treatment. According to Reuter, of the $30 billion now spent annually on drug control (up sharply from $6 to $7 billion in 1985), fully three-quarters is directed at apprehending and punishing dealers and users, while only about one-sixth is going to treatment.

That these particulars read suspiciously like a political liberal's wish list does not make them wrong. Nor does the fact that inner-city drug traffickers are not choirboys mean that imprisoning them is an effective way to deal with the drug problem. The fear of appearing "soft" on the drug issue has had a deleterious effect on the quality of our public debate in this area. As UCLA drug policy expert Mark Kleiman has stressed, drug enforcement differs from other kinds of law enforcement in that "locking up a burglar . . . does not materially change the opportunities for other burglars, while locking up a drug dealer leaves potential customers for new dealers."

The prostitution analogy is apt. Do we really want to pursue a policy—targeting street-level retail dealers for mandatory prison terms—that imposes great costs on a vulnerable part of society while accomplishing little in objective terms? Is this not too high a price to pay in order to provide politicians with a symbol of their righteous determination to "do something" about a problem which, at its root, lies in the consumption habits of the society, rather than in the criminality of its impoverished, urban youth?

Chapter 2

What Are the Effects of Drug Trafficking?

CURRENT CONTROVERSIES

Chapter Preface

Despite the enormous resources poured into the fight against drugs and drug trafficking, officials estimate that the drug supply in America increases by twenty-five hundred tons every year. In 1999 there were an estimated eight thousand agents protecting the border between the United States and Mexico, but officials claim that an average of five to seven tons of marijuana, cocaine, heroin, and methamphetamine enter the United States every day. Drug trafficking along the border has not only increased crime and violence in border cities, but has also negatively affected international trade.

The inception of the North American Free Trade Agreement (NAFTA) in 1994 transformed Mexico into the largest exporter of illicit narcotics to the United States in the world. NAFTA not only opened up trade between Canada, Mexico, and the United States, but also created trade routes for South American drug traffickers. Officials estimate that, because of the enormous flow of legitimate traffic between the two countries, only 10 to 15 percent of the drug flow into the United States is discovered and seized. There were over 4.2 million truck crossings in 1999 alone, which creates a disadvantage for understaffed border patrol agencies. According to a DEA intelligence analyst, "The border is absolutely overwhelmed with numbers—people, vehicles, modes of transportation." Agents cannot inspect every vehicle crossing the border, so drug traffickers successfully export more drugs into the United States than they lose to authorities.

Because of the enormous profits to be made, drug traffickers battle for territory and clientele, resulting in increased crime and violence in such border cities as San Diego and Phoenix. Gang-related crime increases as drug traffickers enlist American gang members as foot soldiers and small-time dealers. Drug-related kidnappings are frequent in small communities. Border patrol agents also contribute to the escalating violence by targeting suspected drug traffickers, often without just cause. In May 1997, an eighteen-year-old goat herder was killed by an unseen U.S. Marine for firing his fifty-year-old .22 caliber rifle, probably to ward off a predator. According to journalist Roberto Suro, "The burgeoning drug traffic from Mexico has generated corruption, violence and a kind of low-intensity war along the 2,000-mile border between Mexico and the United States."

The crime and violence drug trafficking has engendered along the border is one of the issues discussed in the following chapter on the effects of drug trafficking.

Drug Trafficking Contributes to Organized Crime

by Michael T. Horn

About the author: *Michael T. Horn was appointed Director of the National Drug Intelligence Center by the Attorney General of the United States on June 20, 1999.*

Although Colombian traffickers still control and facilitate significant portions of the drug trafficking in the Western Hemisphere, the sophisticated, organized criminal groups from Mexico have eclipsed the drug trafficking criminals from Cali and Medellin, Colombia, as the greatest law enforcement threat facing the United States today. The leaders of these groups—the Rodriguez-Orejuela brothers in Colombia, Juan Garcia-Abrego, Miguel Caro-Quintero, the Arrellano-Felix brothers, and recently deceased Amado Carrillo-Fuentes in Mexico—are simply the 1990s versions of the traditional organized crime leaders that U.S. law enforcement has fought to dismantle since the turn of the century. But the influence of American organized crime pales in comparison to the violence, corruption and power that is exhibited by today's criminal group leaders.

The lifeblood of any organized crime group is corruption, intimidation and violence; which are used to silence and coerce as criminal empires are built. The majority of organized crime is non-ideological. Their motivation is the desire to gain illicit income from a variety of sources. Through the use of raw power and coercion, the members of these organizations strive to keep the body of the group intact and operating in a profitable manner. Organizations often operate on a geographical basis to avoid competition, but when the opportunity for expansion and increased profits presents itself, the leaders of these groups will not hesitate to use any means, from threats to extreme violence, to achieve their goals. . . .

The Violence of the Colombian Cartels

During the 1980s, the Medellin [drug] Cartel held the citizens of Colombia hostage during a reign of terror that threatened to destroy the country, their way

Excerpted from Michael T. Horn's testimony before the U.S. Senate Committee on Foreign Relations, Subcommittee on the Western Hemisphere, Peace Corps, Narcotics, and Terrorism, July 16, 1997.

of life, and their institutions. [The cartel's leader] Pablo Escobar, operating with virtual impunity, went so far as to place bounties on the heads of Colombian National Police officers in the amount of $1,000–$3,000 dollars per murder. The ruthlessness of the Colombian traffickers was imported to the United States as they traveled north to meet the growing demand for cocaine. The violence was first manifested in South Florida, where the violence escalated to such a point that the media began describing the Colombian drug traffickers as the "Cocaine Cowboys". The ability of these powerful organized criminal groups to transport this level of vengeful violence to the U.S. was like nothing that law enforcement had ever experienced before. Failure to perform duties as directed, suspicion of betrayal, or merely the need to set an example, were the rationales for dispensing violence at unprecedented levels. . . .

> *"The lifeblood of any organized crime group is corruption, intimidation and violence."*

During Pablo Escobar's reign as head of the Medellin Cartel, a number of Supreme Court Justices were killed when discussions arose over Colombia's extradition policies. Extradition to the United States and significant jail terms in U.S. prisons is the narco-trafficker's only fear. But as law enforcement pressure increased, and fear of incarceration in American jails became a predominant concern, many of the Colombian traffickers from Medellin fled back to their homeland to establish the headquarters for their immense trafficking empires.

Despite aggressive law enforcement efforts by the Colombian National Police, such powerful trafficking groups still act with impunity, retaining their power through threats, intimidation and murder, directed against rival traffickers, journalists, law enforcement officials, and members of the judicial system.

Colombia still has the highest per capita murder rate in the world, with 24,000 reported murders in 1996. There have also been numerous Colombian National Police Officers killed or injured during the last several years as a result of drug-related violence. Many of these incidents were by the way of car bombings, as well as execution-style murder. In June 1997, in Bogota, eight Colombian National Police Officers were killed and 12 others wounded, when a truck bomb exploded in a precinct parking lot as it was searched for weapons.

While the Medellin Cartel brazenly made a name for itself killing and maiming its foes with car bombs, kidnappings, torture, and automatic weapons, the Cali Cartel leaders were quietly and less brutally taking hold of a large portion of the cocaine trade in a sophisticated, businesslike manner. Their ascension to power was also based on a system of violence and intimidation that was meted out when necessary, but in a far less flamboyant manner.

The Colombian and Mexican Drug Trafficking Alliance

Since the early 1970s, drug traffickers from Colombia had been using the Caribbean corridor and routes through South Florida to smuggle hundreds of tons of cocaine and marijuana into the United States. As a result of their grow-ing notoriety and brazen actions throughout this region, law enforcement atten-tion to the activities of the Colombians intensified. With increased law enforce-ment presence and enforcement in the Caribbean and South Florida, the Colombians were forced to turn to the less sophisticated and structured Mexi-can marijuana traffickers to move their products to growing American markets through Mexico and across the U.S. border.

The Mexican traffickers emulated the methods of operation the Colombians had used successfully for so long. They became more structured in their organizations by adopting the Colombian "cell structure," which compartmentalized and insu-lated each function of the organization. The Mexican transportation organizations began receiving payment for services rendered in the form of cocaine rather than cash, sometimes commanding up to one-half of each shipment being transported across the U.S. border, and turned over to Colombian distribution networks. This arrangement created opportunities for the Mexican trafficking groups to de-velop their own drug distribution net-works and exponentially increase their profits. With this increased wealth came the power to corrupt, intimidate and murder.

> *"Colombia still has the highest per capita murder rate in the world, with 24,000 reported murders in 1996."*

The majority of the cocaine entering the United States continues to come from Colombia through Mexico and across the U.S.-Mexico border. In addition to the inexhaustible supply of cocaine entering the U.S., trafficking organiza-tions from Mexico are responsible for producing and trafficking thousands of pounds of methamphetamine annually. A number of major trafficking organiza-tions represent the highest echelons of organized crime in Mexico. . . .

The Effect of International Organized Crime on the United States

The violence that has long been attendant to the drug trade is evidenced in Mexico, although not yet to the degree that it has been seen in Colombia. In-creasingly, this violence is spilling across the Mexico-U.S. border as traffickers become more brazen and violent in carrying out their mandate of terror and vengeance. The level of violence that is being experienced in Mexico has a di-rect effect on the United States. Violence permeates every level of the trade. The Arrellano-Felix organization is considered the most violent of the Mexican crime families, extending its tentacles from Tijuana to the streets of San Diego. This organization maintains well-armed and well-trained security forces, de-scribed by the Mexican enforcement officials as paramilitary in nature, includ-ing international mercenaries as advisors, trainers and members.

Enforcers are often hired from violent street gangs in cities and towns in both Mexico and the United States in the belief that gang members are expendable.

These members are dispatched to assassinate targeted individuals and send clear messages to those who attempt to utilize the Mexicali/Tijuana corridor without paying the area transit tax demanded by the Arrellano-Felix domain. The Arrellano-Felix organization uses a San Diego based street gang, the "Logan Heights Calle 30," to carry out executions and conduct security for their drug distribution networks. Six members of this group were arrested by DEA and the San Diego Police Department for the murder of a man and his son in San Diego. A total of 49 members of the "Calle 30" have been arrested by the San Diego Task Force on drug trafficking and violent crime charges.

> *"Traffickers [have] become more brazen and violent in carrying out their mandate of terror and vengeance."*

The majority of the 200 murders in Tijuana in 1996 are believed to have been drug-related. There [were] 28 high-profile drug-related assassinations in Mexico from 1993 to 1997: many of these murders remain unsolved. The problem of violence is particularly acute in Mexico. In the February 24, 1997, issue of *U.S. News and World Report*, an article titled "An Inferno Next Door" reports that "Mexico's drug gangs buy the officials they can—and kill those they can't." In a grisly episode, the article tells the story of Hodin Gutierrez, a young prosecutor who was one of eight law enforcement officials to be killed recently in Tijuana. After winning a conviction against a corrupt State police officer and investigating the murder of a police chief who had refused a bribe, Gutierrez was shot 120 times and his killers repeatedly ran their vehicle over his body. These killers were supposedly working for drug traffickers.

In July 1996, the violence along the U.S.-Mexico border exploded, with reports of American property owners under siege by armed traffickers smuggling drugs into the U.S. Fences were destroyed, livestock butchered and random gun shots were fired into homes of ranchers, who reported seeing armed traffickers in Mexico with night vision equipment and communications devices protecting the steady stream of smugglers into the United States. Increased law enforcement presence in these areas has resulted in diminished reports of violence since then, but similar violence in other areas continues.

In 1997, instances of violence directed at U.S. law enforcement also escalated on and around the Southwest border. In April, two Inspectors from the United States Customs Service assigned to the Calexico Point of Entry were shot after directing a marijuana-laden vehicle to secondary inspection. Officers of the United States Border Patrol regularly report receiving rifle fire from residences on the Mexican side of the border. In at least three separate incidents in 1997, Border Patrol Agents have reported receiving fire from Tijuana, and on one occasion in May, a gunman from Mexico fired several rounds from the Mexico side of the San Ysidro Point of Entry, into a U.S. Border Patrol vehicle, injuring the agent.

Violence directed by the Mexican trafficking organizations continues to surge in Mexico, threatening DEA agents, their families and our operations. Threats against DEA and other U.S. officials have escalated in Mexico and along the border. From September 1996, until July 1997, DEA has documented six specific incidents involving agent personnel, two of which have warranted temporary relocation.

Consequently, in September 1996, DEA established the Mexico Threat Assessment Working Group of U.S. law enforcement and intelligence community members. The goal of the Working Group is to ensure that all information on potential threats against either U.S. nationals or host officials in Mexico and along the Southwest Border are consolidated at a single point and handled appropriately. Since its inception, over forty threats against Mexican and U.S. law enforcement officials have been documented. Several of these threats were believed to be serious enough to warrant relocation of affected law enforcement officials from their posts of duty.

The Emergence of New Trafficking Threats

The drug trafficking arena is in a constant state of change; restructuring organizations, adapting to law enforcement efforts, responding to demand, and incorporating new trafficking groups that bring specialties or advantageous distribution networks to the trade. The cocaine trade in the Western Hemisphere, and most specifically the United States, is experiencing its greatest transformation in the last two decades. Due to the largely Mexican-influenced Southwest border area, the Colombian traffickers have pulled back from much of their operations in that part of the United States. They are concentrating their efforts on controlling the cocaine wholesale market in the Eastern United States, Europe, and Asia.

Colombian trafficking groups still maintain a strong-hold on cocaine wholesale and distribution all along the Eastern Seaboard of the United States.

Mexican trafficking organizations now control operations along the U.S.-Mexico border, the Western coast of the U.S. and well into the Midwest of the United States. For the first time, we are seeing Mexican transportation groups delivering quantities of cocaine to Colombian and Dominican trafficking groups in New York City. We also have reports that the Amado Carrillo-Fuentes organization is aggressively seeking to gain a foothold in the lucrative East Coast marketplace. They have adopted the "cell structure" utilized so flawlessly by the Colombians, and have become more disciplined in their operations.

The Caribbean Corridor and the Dominican Factor

In the 1980s, most of the cocaine entering the United States came through the Caribbean and into South Florida. With the Mexican ascension to power and the incarceration of the major Cali drug traffickers, several powerful Colombian organizations and many Cali splinter groups are now returning to the traditional Caribbean routes and are using Puerto Rican and Dominican specialists to transport, distribute and market South American produced marijuana, cocaine, and heroin.

Drug trafficking activities and the violence that accompanies the drug trade increased significantly during the mid-1990s in the Caribbean region. In response, DEA opened its 20th Field Division in San Juan, Puerto Rico in November of 1995. The focus of the Caribbean Field Division is to build prosecutable cases on the leadership of Colombian, Puerto Rican, and Dominican trafficking and smuggling groups that facilitate and control the drug trade throughout the Caribbean corridor.

> *"Violence directed by the Mexican trafficking organizations continues to surge in Mexico, threatening DEA agents, their families and our operations."*

These Colombian crime syndicates have placed an entire command and control infrastructure in the Caribbean, predominantly in Puerto Rico, to direct the movement of cocaine and heroin into the United States, and take advantage of the opportunities that the Caribbean offers. There has been a definitive effort on the part of these Colombian groups to franchise the smuggling and transportation operations to Puerto Rican and Dominican groups in order to minimize their presence in Puerto Rico. This is an example of the recent decentralization of the cocaine trade in Colombia. The leadership of the new Colombian groups is adopting a less monolithic approach in their operations as demonstrated by a willingness to sub-contract transportation services and franchise distribution operations in the United States.

Their organizational structure, therefore, is taking on a somewhat different look than that of their predecessors. The "cell system" is still employed to provide security and compartmentalization, but it no longer exists to the extent that the Colombian traffickers demand complete control over the distribution networks. The Colombian traffickers have cut off the first one or two tiers of the "cell system" and in many cases have been utilizing Dominican trafficking groups to handle, to some degree, wholesale and street level distribution.

Dominican transportation networks use Puerto Rico as the primary staging area for transportation of cocaine and Colombian heroin into the United States. This is an attractive alternative for numerous reasons. The proximity of Puerto Rico to the South American coastline as well as to the U.S. makes it a convenient point for shipment and consolidation of drug loads intended to enter the United States through South Florida or along the East Coast of the U.S. Additionally, the U.S. commonwealth status of Puerto Rico makes it the southernmost point of entry into the U.S. for passengers and goods. Once cargo has cleared Customs on the island, shipping cargo to other areas in the United States from Puerto Rico is considered trade from the interior of the U.S., and is often not subject to further inspection. San Juan handles more than 14 million tons of cargo each year, has the third busiest seaport in North America, and the 14th busiest port in the world. More than 75 daily commercial flights arrive in the Continental United States (CONUS) from Puerto Rico, making it a traffickers paradise due to the sheer volume of commercial trade that takes place in the region.

Equally significant is the large legal and illegal Dominican migration to Puerto Rico that has been increasing steadily over the last several years. Some of these Dominican trafficking groups have gained control of a number of Puerto Rico's housing projects where they utilize violence and intimidation to control the cocaine market. Dominican traffickers have gained a notorious reputation for their disregard for human life. Once the Colombian organizations tranship drug loads into the Caribbean, the Dominican trafficking groups then assume the responsibility for moving the shipment to Puerto Rico and on to the United States, where it is turned over to a Colombian wholesale distribution network, or kept within the Dominican ranks to be sold along the East Coast of the U.S.

Dominican traffickers are clever opportunists who are seeking to further expand and control cocaine trafficking in the northeast corridor of the United States, as well as continue to command a large portion of the market in the Caribbean. The Dominican trafficking groups are no longer merely transporters and low level heroin distributors for the Colombian syndicates, but are expanding their own wholesale distribution networks with Colombian cocaine, and continuing to expand their market share.

Dominican Distribution Networks

Organized criminal groups from Colombia are increasingly relying on Dominican distribution networks to distribute their cocaine at the retail level. These trafficking organizations have now established well-grounded operations which not only distribute cocaine and heroin for the Colombians in the lucrative New York market, but in cities all along the East Coast. Dominican trafficking organizations operate with efficiency. They rely heavily on counter surveillance, and operational security to ensure success for their distribution networks and use sophisticated communications equipment, cloned cellular communications, alarm systems, and police scanners to monitor the activity of law enforcement. They also rely heavily on the ingenious construction of vehicle "traps" to secrete and secure their drug loads for transportation in passenger vehicles or trucks for transportation to cities throughout the Northeast.

"[Puerto Rico is] a trafficker's paradise due to the sheer volume of commercial trade that takes place in the region."

The Dominican traffickers provide a natural conduit for heroin to the large addict population in New York. High quality Colombian heroin can easily be snorted or smoked, rather than injected, which has been the traditional method of administration. Approximately 63 percent of the heroin seized in the United

States last year was of South American origin. The reliability of the established working relationship between the Colombian traffickers and the Dominican transportation groups have proved successful and are currently being used by the Colombians to establish similar heroin trafficking strategies.

Potential Solutions

To shield America's Southwest border the DEA and the FBI launched the Southwest Border Initiative (SWBI) [in 1994], which targets the leaders of the major Mexican trafficking groups that live in Mexico, and control the cocaine, heroin, and methamphetamine on both sides of the border. This strategy is designed to dismantle the sophisticated leadership of these criminal groups from Mexico by targeting their command and control functions and building cases on the surrogate members and their U.S.-based infrastructure. The SWBI is anchored in our belief that the only way to successfully attack any organized crime syndicate is to build strong cases on the leadership and their command and control functions. With the assistance of foreign governments, the long-term incarceration of the leadership will leave entire organizations in disarray. . . .

> *"With the assistance of foreign governments, the long-term incarceration of the leadership will leave entire organizations in disarray."*

Organized criminal groups, whether they are headquartered in Cali or Sonora or the homegrown versions that are predators in our cities and communities, significantly affect the American way of life. The interests and concerns of these heinous criminals lie in the advancement of their criminal enterprises, and wealth that they can derive from plying their trade. They will resort to violence, intimidation, kidnappping, and murder to accomplish their goals.

These international traffickers have acted with impunity for many years and believe that they are beyond the reach of law enforcement. This arrogance extends into their enterprises in the United States. As we have seen with the Arrellano-Felix brothers, these violent traffickers send assassins from Mexico into San Diego to exact their revenge on those who do not pay their drug debt or who cooperate with our efforts to put an end to their reign of terror. The brazen attacks on American law enforcement along our Southwest border and in our cities and towns must not be tolerated and must continue to be met with coordinated investigative strategies that will ultimately lead to the demise of international organized crime and its destructive influence on our streets.

Applying a multi-agency approach to attack these organized trafficking groups will continue to be our strongest asset in dismantling the organized criminal syndicates that control the drug trade in the U.S. We must continue working with foreign counterparts to target the upper echelon criminal leaders, as well as their surrogates who bring violence to our communities as they sell poison to our children.

Drug Trafficking Contributes to Gang-Related Crime

by the Drug Enforcement Administration

About the author: *The Drug Enforcement Administration is a government agency that strives to decrease the amount of drugs traded and consumed in the United States and in neighboring countries.*

Throughout the United States, low-level dealing in drugs is being increasingly handled by violent and highly organized criminal gangs. There are three major types of gangs involved in street sales of drugs: prison gangs, traditional street gangs, and outlaw motorcycle gangs.

Prison Gangs

Since prison gangs operate in a detached environment, the DEA is limited in its ability to target them. But the DEA will often target associates who assist in the drug trafficking process and are not currently incarcerated.

Prison gangs are organized generally along racial lines. They were originally formed by prisoners to protect themselves from other inmates. For example, the Mexican Mafia was established in 1957 at the Deuel Vocational Center in Tracy, California, by Hispanic inmates to counter pressure from African-American inmates. Today, through an elaborate network of distributors and dealers, it controls part of the drug trade in Southern California.

The Black Guerilla Family had its origins in the black power movement of the 1960s. It was organized at California's San Quentin State Penitentiary in 1966. Today the Black Guerillas distribute heroin and cocaine to the California street gangs under its influence. Another San Quentin gang later became known as the Aryan Brotherhood and adopted an ideology of white supremacy. Currently, its primary interest is distributing drugs.

Two prison factions developed in the Illinois penal system: the People Nation

Reprinted from the Drug Enforcement Administration's publication "Domestic Trafficking Gangs," 2000, found at www.usdoj.gov/dea/traffickers/domestic.htm.

and the Folks Nation. Two gangs under the rubric of the People Nation, the Vice Lords and the Latin Kings, are dedicated to the preservation of Latin heritage and distribute drugs in their respective neighborhoods. Prominent among the Folks Nation are the Black Gangster Disciples, a gang that has been a target of the DEA in recent years. Theories on what "Folks" is an acronym for vary. Some members interpret the name as "Follow and Obey all Laws of Kings," others call themselves "Followers of Lord King Satan."

Street and Motorcycle Gangs

Many street gangs confine their drug trafficking activities to their own neighborhoods. However, several gangs have gone national. Such "supergangs" are hard to distinguish from major organized crime groups. For example, two supergangs, the Crips and the Bloods, have their origin in Los Angeles in the late 1960s. At first, their activities were limited to large urban areas. But these two gangs now have more than 1,000 affiliates in more than 100 cities. Many of the affiliates are "cultural" rather than "structural," meaning they take a gang's recognizable name but are not necessarily associated with other chapters. Almost half of these cities with Crips and Bloods associates are small to midsize, with populations of less than 100,000. Because drugs often yield much higher profits in small cities and in rural areas than they do in big cities, members of both gangs have moved to smaller cities and set up distribution networks that reach back to their counterparts in the large cities and

> *"Through an elaborate network of distributors and dealers, [the Mexican Mafia] controls part of the drug trade in Southern California."*

sometimes to the major international trafficking groups. Street gangs frequently have ties to prison gangs. Leaders are often former prisoners and take their orders from fellow gang members still in prison.

Outlaw motorcycle gangs emerged following World War II. At first, they focused on riding motorcycles and throwing wild parties, but they increasingly turned to violence. In 1947, a group of outlaw bikers attending a motorcycle rally destroyed the town of Hollister, California, when one of its members was arrested. The biker gangs gradually moved into criminal pursuits, often working closely with the traditional mafia. Today the four major biker gangs are the Hells Angels, the Outlaws, the Bandidos, and the Pagans. A significant source of income for most biker gangs is drug trafficking, especially the manufacture and distribution of methamphetamine.

Gang Activities

Although there is considerable debate over what constitutes a gang, there are several characteristics that seem to be common to the criminal gangs mentioned above. Many of these modern gangs are highly organized, they exhibit a willingness to use violence to accomplish their objectives, and they rely heavily on drug trafficking for their major source of income.

Gangs like the Gangster Disciples, the Latin Kings, and Hells Angels are far more organized than the term "gang" might suggest. Many gangs have a structured hierarchy, complete with presidents, vice presidents, and secretary treasurers. But they are not as dependent upon their leadership as traditional organized crime families. Quite often a gang will continue to function even after its leaders have been convicted and imprisoned. New members are carefully screened to determine whether they meet the personality traits needed for the violent, secretive world of gang life. Prospective Hells Angels often take polygraph tests and are required to commit a witnessed felony in order to prove their loyalty, thus making it extremely difficult for undercover law enforcement officers to infiltrate the organization.

> *"A significant source of income for most biker gangs is drug trafficking, especially the manufacture and distribution of methamphetamine."*

The nature of their criminal enterprises forces them to create relationships with other criminal organizations, particularly those who distribute the illegal drugs. They frequently meet with other gangs to carve up markets, arrange for the sharing of drug shipments, pool money for buying large shipments of drugs, and negotiate disputes. Some of the larger street gangs have international connections with suppliers in Colombia, Mexico, Nigeria, Pakistan, and other countries. The secretive nature of their operations forces them to develop a tight "command and control" structure. The profits they make from the drug trade enable them to invest in highly sophisticated technology, such as encryption devices to conceal their communications and a variety of telecommunications equipment to keep them in constant contact with their suppliers and with each other.

Armed and Dangerous

Gangs also use weapons to protect their turf and their drug operations from one another. There was a time when gang members relied on switchblade knives and homemade zip guns. Today, the huge profits from drug trafficking have given gangs access to well-stocked arsenals of sophisticated arms, including semiautomatic military assault weapons, .50 caliber machine guns, and a variety of explosives. Along with the sophisticated weapons comes a willingness to use them. In fact, it is impossible to join or get ahead in many gangs without committing a certifiable crime, sometimes including homicide. La Nuestra Familia, a gang of Mexican-American convicts, even keeps their own "Ten Most Wanted List." One can become a "captain" or a "general" in the organization by murdering someone on the list.

Gangs who, in effect, take over towns and neighborhoods are often able to maintain their drug distribution networks by demonstrating their superior firepower and their commitment to use violence to achieve their ends. Gangs have been noted for using violence against witnesses, law enforcement officers, and prosecutors. A Hells Angels motto, for example, sums up that organization's cavalier attitude about violence: "Three people can keep a secret, if two are dead."

Many of the criminal gangs involved in drug trafficking have followed a similar pattern: what starts as a loosely organized outlet for school dropouts and social misfits becomes a tightly organized criminal enterprise. Among their many criminal activities are murder-for-hire, auto theft, extortion, prostitution, and insurance fraud.

But no activity is more profitable than drug trafficking. Because they have every incentive to spend most of their time and energies on the most profitable part of their business, modern street gangs have become, to a great extent, smaller versions of the large, international drug groups with whom they do business. The huge amounts of money that pour in from the drug trade corrupt the communities in which the gangs live. Ten-year-olds have been known to make several hundred dollars a week just for being lookouts for crack cocaine houses. The enormous profits raise the stakes in the drug trade, leading to violent battles over turf. The profits also finance the purchase of sophisticated weaponry and communications technology, often overwhelming law enforcement agencies in smaller jurisdictions.

Drug Trafficking Harms America's Youth

by Colbert I. King

About the author: *Colbert I. King serves as a deputy editorial page editor at the* Washington Post.

The cold statistics produced by the Washington, D.C. Pretrial Services Agency have an almost numbing quality.

Fifty-four juveniles, age 16, were arrested in December 1999. Thirty-two of them, or 59 percent, tested positive for drugs. Thirty-two 15-year-olds were also arrested; 19 of them, or 59 percent, had drugs in their system. Another piece of data: A 12-year-old apprehended by police also tested positive for drugs.

November 1999 wasn't any better. No, it was worse. Of 49 16-year-olds taken into police custody, 71 percent tested positive for cocaine, marijuana or PCP; 22 15-year-olds placed under arrest also tested positive for drugs.

One November entry jumps off the page: Two 10-year-old children arrested—one tested positive for drugs.

Would that only one arrested preadolescent turned up with drugs in his system in 1999. Not by a long shot. There was a 12-year-old in October, a 10-year-old in September, two 12-year-olds in July, one 11-year-old in June, two 12-year-olds in May, one 10-year-old in April, one 12-year-old in March, one 10-year-old in February and one 12-year-old in January. All tested positive for drugs.

These statistics reflect drug usage among juveniles arrested and tested prior to their initial court hearings. They say nothing about children and teenagers outside the criminal justice system who are using marijuana, cocaine and PCP. It's a safe bet, however, that illegal drug use isn't confined to only those who've been busted.

Steady Statistics

And don't think for a moment that the November and December 1999 statistics are some kind of anomaly. Check this out. The detection of drugs in the

Excerpted from "Ten-Year-Olds on Drugs," by Colbert I. King, *The Washington Post*, February 5, 2000; © 2000, The Washington Post. Reprinted with permission.

systems of arrested juveniles has been relatively constant over the past five years. The percentages of arrested juveniles testing positive for drugs from 1995 through 1999 tell the story: 60 percent in 1995; 64 percent in '96; 64 percent in '97; 64 percent in '98; and 65 percent in '99. In fact, according to the agency's most recent report, year-end totals of PCP use among arrested juveniles increased from 1998 to 1999. So did marijuana use. Only cocaine use decreased from 1998 to 1999—by one percentage point.

Enough with the numbers. Where am I headed with this?

Think back carefully. When was the last time you heard anyone in a position of responsibility in this city, from the mayor to the council, from preacher to business or labor leader, call for a serious and sustained public campaign against the scourge of drugs on the youth—and soul—of this city.

Yet it's hard to identify a more corrupting element in the District.

A *Washington Post* story in February 2000 on the police department's latest crusade against open-air drug markets offered a glimpse into the damage that illegal drugs, and those who deal them, are inflicting on the next generation.

The piece showed what a number of us have seen or have suspected was going on in some of our neighborhoods: Young children and teenagers serving as lookouts for drug hustlers, tipping them off by phones or beepers when the police are spotted; drug dealers buying loyalty and protection by bribing kids with trinkets and slipping cash to their mothers.

Drug dealers not only are defiling our communities; they are corrupting our children. Imagine—boys and girls as young as 5 or 6 years old being taught that the police, not drug peddlers, are the ones to watch out for; that helping people break the law or lying in their defense is okay if it gets you some money in return; that cash is king and everything else is a distant second.

Political Rhetoric

And what's being done about it? Virtually nothing. Irresponsible parents who are letting the streets raise their children are allowed to wriggle off the hook with alibis about being stressed out by the woes of daily living or some such rot. ("Careful now, we don't want to injure their self-esteem.")

Politicians know they don't make themselves popular, and pastors know it doesn't help the collection plate, when they start hammering at the destructive conduct that is tolerated in some of our communities. They keep

> *"It's a safe bet . . . that illegal drug use isn't confined to only those who've been busted."*

their disapproval to themselves—except in the privacy of their homes or when they are among friends. Better to utter platitudes and get on with it.

As for children from homes where adult supervision and discipline are missing and disrespect for authority is spawned, we mandate that they be dispatched to public school each day for principals and teachers to somehow "fix."

Oh, but it would be false to say this is a city that doesn't care, that can't get fired up.

Just let some issue with potentially juicy overtones of color and class come along—such as replacing an elected school board with an appointed panel [as Washington, D.C., unsuccessfully proposed in 2000]—and watch as the adrenaline starts pumping in our demagogues, racial paranoiacs and conspiracy theorists. As a city, we can sure get into that stuff.

Even as loads of our children are going to hell.

Drug Trafficking Harms Inner Cities

by Jamie Dettmer

About the author: *Jamie Dettmer is a senior editor for politics and investigative news at* Insight, *a semimonthly conservative news magazine.*

The lost souls are out tonight. Again. They're out every night. Every day. On street corners fronting boarded-up row houses. In alleyways between ugly, squat projects. They slouch. They loiter. They shuffle in their Babylon with dying eyes in the dead of night, their youth imprisoned in wrecked bodies. They become really alert for only two things—for a passing squad car or a dealer and the chance to score so they can snort, smoke, mainline or chase the poison—cocaine, heroin, marijuana—that's shattered their lives into biochemical shards. And behind them, incredibly, looms the dome of the Congress of the United States of America—the ultimate symbol of the shining city on the hill.

In the corridors of congressional power, a mere 10 minutes away from the night of the living dead, [presidential] officials, lawmakers and their aides debate policies that are meant to free the lost souls, to find a place for even those shards in the mosaic of the American Dream. There's talk of strategies for demand-reduction or supply-reduction, about whether a rehabilitation-led approach is the way to go, or fierce interdiction or drug education is the answer.

But down at this level—the streets of Southeast Washington, the stash houses, the cravings, the lives without purpose, the derelict women selling what's left of themselves, the squad cars and overworked, overwhelmed police—down here, the nearby political rhetoric seems just so much talk.

Street War on Drugs

Down here it is low-intensity warfare, an unglamorous, messy, depressing battle fought block by block, day after day, night after long, red-eyed night. And if the enemy is the addict or the hooked peon earning their score by selling drugs to others, it's a pathetic enemy indeed, one who pleads with resignation,

Excerpted from "Capital Shame," by Jamie Dettmer, *Insight*, July 6–13, 1998. Copyright 1998 News World Communications, Inc. All rights reserved. Reprinted with the permission of *Insight*.

"Please don't do that," when an officer arrests him and seizes his $10 bags of coke. It's an enemy that whines and wheedles and begs, but for all of that a dangerous foe, one who suddenly can flash a loaded gun. The street addicts—the most visible part of the drug trade—even fear each other: "I'm not afraid of the police or the gangs," says a crack addict who lives on the street. "I'm afraid of the other addicts—they'll choke you, strangle you, knife you, shoot you, they'll do anything to get your dope."

"We're losing," says a veteran district cop, [during] an off-duty tour of some of the roughest streets in the nation's capital. "A year ago I thought we were winning. We were getting some real good busts. Now it's going wild again. We can lock up little Billy who stands selling on a street corner but there'll be another little Billy and then another."

Since the 1960s Washington has been one of the country's most lucrative urban narcotics markets. Three decades ago heroin was the drug of choice and, although the market basically was disorganized, there was a line of major dealers and wholesalers who dominated sales—men such as Lawrence "Slippery" Jackson, who purchased his smack from New York's Italian dons and shipped it to the district by car and Amtrak for re-cutting and street distribution, and James "Dumptruck" Smith, who was considered a gentleman by the cops who eventually arrested him.

The Crack Cocaine Menace

In the 1980s, when crack cocaine hit, the city turned meaner and more violent—the twenty-something and younger generation of native dealers who emerged fought viciously for turf and waged a bloody conflict to drive off trespassing Jamaican gangs from New York and Miami. The death toll soared, turning Washington into the "murder capital" of the United States. The city's drug problem shifted from being a local story into an international scandal—one made more sensational with the presence of a crack-head mayor, Marion Barry, whose antipathy toward the police and his own fear of investigation resulted in one of the nation's finest police forces being cut back, neutered and, some say, ruined.

Washington became a symbolic test of the nation's progress—or lack of it—in the war on drugs. George Bush used it as a backdrop for his 1989 "the-rules-of-the-game-have-changed" speech in which he warned the South American cartels that there was a new sheriff. Then-drug czar Bill Bennett

"Down at this [street] level . . . the nearby political rhetoric seems just so much talk."

set out to make an example of the capital by showing what federal resolve and greenbacks could do. But after pumping a few million dollars into a federal task force and reneging on a promise to build state-of-the-art treatment centers, there wasn't much to show for the effort except for an increase in convictions, overflowing jails and more drugs and mayhem in the streets of the district.

So how's the capital doing now, nearly three years after a federal control board was introduced to take over the running of much of the city's government? Is the capital an example other U.S. cities can take pride in and look up to as a role model?

Some Good News

There have been some recent successes on the law-enforcement front. In 1998, the local police, with support from federal agencies, broke a drug network that reached from Colombia to Washington to a federal prison in Lewisburg, Pa., where the infamous Rayful Edmond III had been held since he was convicted in 1989 of running one of the city's largest trafficking outfits. In exchange for a lighter prison term for his mother, Constance D. "Bootsie" Perry, who was serving a 14-year sentence for her narcotics dealing in the 1980s, Edmond turned informant and ratted on up-and-coming drug wholesalers Rodney Murphy and Jimmy J. Robinson. From his prison cell, Edmond had linked the ambitious pair with Medellin cartel figures Osvaldo Trujillo-Blanco and his brother Dixon Dario Trujillo-Blanco, earning $200,000 in the bargain, according to reports. Edmond's cooperation resulted in his mother's early release from federal prison June 2, 1998.

Around the same time, district police and federal agents arrested, on charges of drug distribution and conspiracy, 20 members of the Seventh and O Street Crew, also known as the Kennedy Dog-Pound Crew, a violent outfit that supplied the Shaw neighborhood in Northwest Washington. Among those apprehended were three men who accompanied the convicted killer of popular Washington cop Brian T. Gibson the night the officer was murdered in February 1996.

> *"Washington became a symbolic test of the nation's progress—or lack of it—in the war on drugs."*

District U.S. attorneys and the city's top cops were right to hail both the Murphy and Robinson convictions and the arrests of the Kennedy Dog-Pound Crew as significant. But were they turning points?

No one had the audacity to make that claim. In welcoming the June crackdown on the Seventh and O Street Crew, U.S. Attorney Wilma A. Lewis stopped short of talking about breakthroughs. In an official statement at the time of the arrests she said: "For too long, the actions of this group have made it difficult for the residents of this area to live a normal and safe life. We can only hope that beginning today the residents of the Seventh and O Street neighborhood can begin to reclaim their streets." Assistant Police Chief Rodney Monroe also mentioned aspirations. "Hopefully this operation will take a major supplier of drugs off of the streets. We hope now to sustain the actions of enforcement to keep this off of the streets."

Keep hope alive is the message. Old-timers in the police try to do so, but many local lawmen expressed deep pessimism about the course the war on drugs is taking in the city. From their perspective, the challenge is overwhelming, and the recent decision to shift more officers into high-visibility, community-policing roles may be compounding the problem. With scarce resources, the community policing has come at a cost—50 percent cuts in the narcotics branch and vice squads.

> *"With scarce resources, the community policing has come at a cost—50 percent cuts in the narcotics branch and vice squads."*

A 1998 multiagency threat assessment for Washington outlines the challenge in stark, bureaucratic prose and paints a bleak narcotics future for the city. The first page of the 50-page report states among other things that:

- "The availability of high-purity heroin is on the rise";
- "Available data indicate that marijuana is on the rise with juveniles/young adults perceiving marijuana as less harmful";
- While use of crack and powdered cocaine by adults is believed to have peaked, that isn't the case with juveniles in low-income neighborhoods; and
- "Juvenile drug distribution, drug transportation, violent crime and gang involvement are increasing."

The result? Drug-related murder rates jumped by 10 percent from 1995 to 1998. And with the increase in juvenile drug use and gang involvement that rate won't fall anytime soon.

The Threat of Gangs

As with many U.S. cities, most neighborhood drug distribution in Washington is carried out by street gangs. In Washington they're known as crews and tend to be loosely structured, family-based groups tied to particular streets or open-air drug markets. Because all the members are either related, were classmates or are neighbors, undercover infiltration is virtually impossible. Police have to rely on informants informing on rival crews or on painstaking so-called "buy-and-identify" operations involving months of purchasing drugs and developing a mosaic of a crew's pattern—where drug stash houses may be, where bank records and lists of beeper numbers may be kept.

Of the 300 or so estimated crews in the district, 199 are involved in narcotics, states the multiagency threat assessment. As well as the crews, there are another eight criminal groups working in the district that are deemed "major drug-trafficking organizations," some with ties to South American, Nigerian and Jamaican cartels.

And the crews again are getting more confident and brazen, though not yet on the scale of the late eighties when Southeast Washington's spectacular murder sprees made Northern Ireland's Belfast look mellow. As with the eighties, so with the nineties. The 15- to 25-year-olds who lead and man the crews are as dedicated to the gun and as impressed as their predecessors were with easy cash—even a small five- to 10-strong crew can make about $5,000 a day. "They live all that old TV stuff—John Wayne, Al Capone," says a narcotics detective. . . .

Wholesalers

The trafficking pecking order doesn't stop with the crews. According to a highly experienced local narcotics sergeant, there probably are more than 1,000 individual drug wholesalers in the district and the suburbs of Northern Virginia and Southern Maryland. Some are small-timers earning a few hundred thousand dollars a year; top ones can bring in $5 million to $6 million annually. Again, some have direct links with international crime syndicates. . . .

The wholesalers are at the level undercover cops are keen to infiltrate—it is a strategic level from which trails can be followed to New York and the South American cartels. But given the anonymous nature of most wholesalers, their discretion and low profiles, penetration poses tough challenges. The wholesalers fall into two camps: those who come from somewhere else in the United States or overseas and had drug connections before they arrived to set up shop, and ambitious, bright crew members. The latter can be identified more easily, though they tend to make the transfer after having served a jail term. Says an undercover narc, "Once they've been to jail, they've been to college—and they move out to the suburbs."

Wholesaler busts are rare and more often than not are fortuitous rather than planned. A few years ago one major wholesaler was identified when a fire broke out in his main stash house—police stumbled onto a store of 500 kilograms [1,100 pounds] of cocaine. Edmonds' mistake was trying to straddle both the worlds of wholesaling and crew-running—his profile, particularly with the killings he was involved in, was too high. . . .

Lack of Funding

Congress also has earned the scorn of district drug fighters. Although Congress has authority over antinarcotics funding, and despite complaints it has not done enough to take matters into its own hands, it has not funded the needed expansion of narcotics enforcement. This raises charges of hypocrisy.

> *"Given the anonymous nature of most wholesalers, their discretion and low profiles, penetration poses tough challenges."*

The same goes for getting to grips with the transportation networks that move narcotics into the district. Washington poses particular challenges on that front. The city and its suburbs are well-served with interstate highways, there are three major airports—two of them international—and a nearby seaport in Baltimore. . . .

There are other areas of neglect. Drugs aren't just a black problem. White

Washington on the west side of Rock Creek Park, the green line that separates affluence from poverty, probably has more drugs, say narcotics cops. And more cash to spend on them. On Friday and Saturday nights when the capital's Northwest clubs and bars are swinging, buying narcotics is as easy as getting a latte from Starbucks. Cocaine, heroin, marijuana and ecstasy can all be bought.

But white arrests are unusual. Black street-dealers east of Rock Creek Park complain of racism. "I say to them," says a sergeant, "You are out there and you're flashing it—if I see a white doing it, I'll shove him in jail, too." In fact, discrete street-dealing by whites on major corners isn't as rare as it once was. Despite that, the main antinarcotics focus remains on the eastern side of the city. Because of the homicides and the street visibility, the public clamors for action. But it is white money—from the suburbs—that makes Washington such a lucrative market, as a ride down Southeast's H Street, known as the Strip, testifies. The tags on the cars of the buyers? Virginia and Maryland.

Drug Trafficking Harms International Trade

by Ken Dermota

About the author: *Ken Dermota is a Knight Foundation journalism fellow in Santiago, where he is analyzing the news media in modern Chile.*

Back in 1993, I had coffee with one of Pablo Escobar's [the leader of the notorious Medellín drug cartel] men. He's dead now (or at least pretending to be), so I suppose I can tell you his name was Juan Fernando Toro. As we sat in a corner restaurant in Medellín, Colombia, Toro was writing excitedly on a napkin.

"Look! Now that the border is open to Venezuela, I can nearly double my profits! I can buy a kilo of cocaine—a good one, made with ether and acetone—for $1,200." He jotted a quick balance sheet on the napkin: Transport of a kilo of cocaine to New York on a small plane, $8,000. Sale price in New York, $18,000. Profit, $8,800.

"Now, I make a lot more money if I send that same kilo through Venezuela," Toro said, scribbling: Transport to Maracaibo or Caracas, $600. Shipment to New York, $2,000. Profit, $14,200. . . .

Things were going to get even better, said Toro. César Galviria, who was then Colombia's president, was negotiating a free trade pact with Mexico and Venezuela. "Soon, I'll be able to ship through Mexico right to the U.S.!" Toro said with childlike enthusiasm. . . .

Unfortunately for him, Toro was killed by enemies of Pablo Escobar before he could prove his point. The rest of the infamous "Medellín cartel" was similarly dismembered, and so it was the Cali group of traffickers that went on to make the Mexican connection. Just months after the North American Free Trade Agreement (NAFTA) came into force, on January 1, 1994, 80 percent of the cocaine for the U.S. market was entering the country through Mexico, according to the U.S. Drug Enforcement Administration (DEA).

Then I understood Toro's strategy. It was not that Mexicans were better smugglers than the Colombians, nor that Mexican officials were more corrupt. In

Excerpted from "Snow Business," by Ken Dermota, *World Policy Journal*, Winter 1999/2000. Reprinted with permission.

economic jargon, the Mexican traffickers' comparative advantage was in the free trade agreement with the United States.

Anything NAFTA did to facilitate regional trade would also stimulate the trade in drugs. Not only did the increased amount of cargo crossing the U.S.-Mexico border provide lots of nooks and crannies in which to hide drugs, but NAFTA's international capital flows made the search for drug profits the equivalent of looking for a needle in a haystack.

The only thing that distinguishes the drug trade from any other kind of trade is its illegality. Declaring drugs to be illegal does not alter the laws of supply and demand, especially when they apply to the world's most profitable business. The United States found out the hard way that there is no invisible hand at the border that sorts out cocaine from cargo and laundered money from investment capital.

The Mexican Conundrum

In 1995, a year after NAFTA joined the United States, Canada, and Mexico into one market, then DEA administrator Thomas A. Constantine reported that Mexican traffickers "have developed and maintained control of the U.S. markets for heroin, cocaine and amphetamines in the U.S." That same year, the State Department reported, "No country in the world poses a more immediate narcotics threat to the United States than Mexico."

By 1996, Mexico had become Latin America's second largest cultivator of opium poppies, after Colombia. Colombians were shipping cocaine to Mexico in loads as large as eight tons in Boeing 727s and Caravelles. By 1997, "Mexican drug syndicates . . . [had] divided up the territory with the Colombian organizations, gradually assuming responsibility for the wholesale distribution of most of the cocaine moving to the United States," according to the State Department. "Mexico now rivals Colombia as the center of the Western Hemisphere drug trade." How did this happen so quickly? . . .

In the crucial period straddling the inception of NAFTA, Mexico's imports of legal goods from Colombia increased from $17 million in 1990 to $121 million in 1995, while Mexico's trade with the United States doubled. Clearly, the increased trade provided more opportunities for Colombian traffickers to piggyback their cocaine

> *"The only thing that distinguishes the drug trade from any other kind of trade is its illegality."*

onto shipments into Mexico. In 1995, I asked the American ambassador to Colombia, Miles Frechette, if the United States hadn't seen that one coming. He replied in writing:

> It was felt by those who supported the NAFTA and by the Bill Clinton Administration that using the argument that any increase in trade could increase drug trafficking and money laundering was not a sufficient argument to over-

come the need of the United States for increasing markets for its exports abroad and also to engage in greater trade with countries of the region.

The United States simply could not square the circle. It was American policy to promote legitimate business in Colombia and the rest of the Andean Group as an alternative to drug trafficking. The Andean Trade Preference Act gave tariff-free entry to 80 percent of the items Colombia exports to the United States. The World Bank, the International Monetary Fund, and U.S. officials recommended that Colombia "modernize" its economy by lowering tariffs, removing import restrictions, and facilitating the free flow of capital in and out of the country. However, once Colombia complied, the DEA published a paper excoriating it for doing those things. Why? Because privatizing its banks, improving capital flows and infrastructure facilitated the drug trade. . . .

Nonetheless, U.S. officials went ahead with NAFTA, ignoring the possible consequences, because trade had priority. NAFTA contains no language to counteract its inherent benefits to drug traffickers. So as NAFTA helped make Mexico into a $130 billion trading partner with the United States, putting it on a par with Japan, it facilitated illegitimate businesses as well.

Keeping Mum

U.S. law enforcement officials were told to keep mum about globalization's seamy side. "We restrained our comments on NAFTA. It was a hot potato we were not supposed to touch, no question [about it]," said Phil Jordan, who, until January 1996 was director of the DEA's El Paso Intelligence Center. Jordan called NAFTA "a godsend" to Mexican traffickers and "the best thing that happened to product distribution since Nike signed up Michael Jordan." U.S. drug and customs agents were soon referring to the "North American Drug Trade Agreement," as they watched the number of trucks and railroad cars crossing the border from Mexico rise to 3.5 million a year.

> *"NAFTA contains no language to counteract its inherent benefits to drug traffickers."*

The freight crossing the U.S. border with Mexico annually weighs about 400 million tons. The number of trucks making the crossing in and of itself is not the problem; it's what is in their secret compartments, as drug smugglers get ever more sophisticated about moving their product. "They have very specific issues," notes Craig Chretien, a special agent in the DEA's San Diego office. "Does a perishable get through quicker than a load of steel?" Smugglers have even been known to sacrifice a smaller load to distract customs agents while a larger load is spirited through. . . .

More rigorous inspections would slow trade to a crawl, as the Nixon administration found out in 1969. In one of the opening salvos of the "drug war," the administration decided to try to stop the flow of marihuana into the United States by checking every vehicle coming in from Mexico. As a result of Operation Intercept, traffic backed up for miles and the Mexican border was nearly closed. The operation was called off after 19 days amid howls of protest from importers. With the border open to trade, the only way to stop the influx of drugs is with gun-slinging law enforcement. . . .

The Allure of Profit

The temptation that Latin Americans succumb to is the temptation of money. It is inconceivable that people in a developing country would not be attracted to the huge profits offered by drug trafficking.

The figures speak for themselves. The retail price of a gram of cocaine on the streets of New York is just under $100. Generally, however, the cocaine sold on the streets is only 50 percent pure. The retail price of a pure gram of cocaine in Colombia is about one U.S. dollar. So, the real price of that gram of cocaine in New York is 200 times the selling price in Colombia. With those givens, the rest of the drug trafficking story is really just commentary. No other product returns 20,000 percent on investment, divided among various middlemen along the way. So long as U.S. consumers are willing to pay 200 times the real price of a manufactured good, some poor Latino with an urge to get ahead is going to make sure that it gets to the streets of New York.

What creates the price difference? Each border crossed entails risk. At each point along the way, those people taking the risk demand to be compensated, whether they are smugglers or paid-off members of a law enforcement agency. It is its illegality that makes the drug trade so lucrative—and so violent. Traffickers would soon be out of business if the drugs were legalized, and there would be no reason to defend the trade with assault weapons.

It is a lot to ask of Mexicans to stop the world's most lucrative business. Mexican police, judges, and investigators are paid Third World wages (in pesos) and so are easily corrupted with First World bribes (in dollars). Antinarcotics police have been corrupted and wind up protecting the traffickers who, after all, can pay a lot more than the government does. Mexicans have seen photographs and news videotape of street dealers in American cities peddling their wares with impunity. The United States seems to live with the drug trade, they say, so why shouldn't Mexico? If you want to find somebody to blame, look where the *real* money is made—on the U.S. side of the border, not in Mexico or Colombia. . . .

Trade Is Trade

Captain America and Billy financed their cross country adventure in the film *Easy Rider* with the sale of a single kilogram of cocaine. Back then, in the late 1960s, a kilogram of cocaine was worth $250,000. In today's money, that would come to three times as much, or $750,000. However, at today's wholesale price of $18,000, Captain America and Billy would not be able pay for one of their Harley-Davidson choppers. Richard Nixon, who was president then, declared the "war on drugs." In the years since, we have spent upward of $40 billion on narcotics enforcement and interdiction, and on crop substitution programs, but illegal drugs are cheaper and more plentiful than ever. Still, the drug warriors battle on, with the same mentality that prevailed during the Vietnam War: the cure for a failing strategy is more of it.

The United States refuses to see what even Pablo Escobar understood. "If there are no consumers, there are no traffickers," he told me in a letter Juan Fernando Toro delivered that day in the coffee shop in Medellín. The United States is the purchaser of most of the illicit drugs produced in Latin America. In a monopsony—where there is only one buyer—it is much easier to attack the demand side. The State Department, in its own way, has recognized the Sisyphean nature of the drug war: "Even the 20 metric tons or so of cocaine that the United States government and its Western Hemisphere partners typically seize in a year have little discernible effect on the price or availability. The combination of strong demand and extraordinary profits continue to make the U.S. the cocaine syndicates' foremost market.

No matter where you stand on the issue of illegal drugs, whether you want to raise the criminal penalties or you believe our jails are full enough; or if you want to decriminalize, legalize, or bomb Colombia off the map, a coherent drug policy must begin with the premise that trade in drugs is still trade.

Drug Trafficking Harms the Economy

by Bruce Zagaris and Scott Ehlers

About the author: *Bruce Zagaris, an attorney, is founder and editor of the In-*ternational Enforcement Law Reporter. *Scott Ehlers is the director of research with the Campaign for New Drug Policies.*

The trade in illicit drugs is estimated to be worth $400 billion a year, or 8% of all international trade. In order to invest the profits of their illicit activities and avoid having their assets seized by the government, drug traffickers must transform the monetary proceeds from their criminal activity into revenue from apparently legal sources. This is known as money laundering.

Though there are many ways to launder drug money, the process generally involves three basic stages. The first stage, placement, entails depositing the drug proceeds into domestic and foreign financial institutions. The second stage, layering, involves creating layers between the persons placing the proceeds and the persons involved in the intermediary stages, to hide their source and ownership and to disguise the audit trail. This can involve complex manipulations and the use of wire transfers, shell companies, bearer shares, and nominees in offshore financial centers (OFCs). In the third stage, integration, the proceeds have been washed, and a legitimate explanation for the funds is created. This can be done, for instance, via front companies, false invoicing, the purchase of financial instruments (stocks, bonds, and certificates of deposit), or investment in real estate, tourism, and other legitimate businesses.

Launderers have devised an infinite number of schemes to hide the large sums that are generated by illicit drug sales. One method, structuring, involves breaking up large amounts of cash into transactions that each amount to less than $10,000 to avoid currency reporting requirements. Other laundering schemes involve casinos, gems and precious metals, wire transfer companies, and smuggling currency out of the United States. The enormous profitability of drug trafficking enables criminals to take advantage of the balloon effect of transna-

Reprinted, with permission, from "Drug Trafficking and Money Laundering," by Bruce Zagaris and Scott Ehlers, *Foreign Policy in Focus*, vol. 6, no. 18 (May 2001), found at www.fpif.org/briefs/vol6/v6n18launder_body.html.

tional contraband trade. As soon as law enforcement officials identify and act to block one laundering method, criminals switch methods, industries, geographic routes, intermediaries, technologies, and so forth. These wealthy and powerful drug syndicates employ professionals and use the latest technology, intelligence, and methods, including buying influence in smaller countries, so that they are always a step or two ahead of law enforcement.

Fighting Back

Since 1970, a series of U.S. laws and directives have sought to scrutinize suspicious financial activities and criminalize deceptive cash transactions. The 1986 Money Laundering Control Act declared money laundering to be a crime in its own right and made structuring to avoid currency reporting a criminal offense. In 1995, then President Bill Clinton announced an initiative and signed Presidential Decision Directive 42, which freezes U.S. assets of Colombian drug trafficking organizations and bars U.S. companies from doing business with the traffickers' front companies. However, a number of other countries have questioned this approach, and no other country has yet agreed to adopt this U.S. initiative.

In 1999, the U.S. enacted the Foreign Narcotics Kingpin Designation Act, which extends the directive to cover kingpins of all nationalities and requires U.S. banks and financial institutions to apply a complex web of economic sanctions against kingpins and their associates. In practice, U.S. financial institutions are required to install and monitor software to detect names of individuals and entities on the kingpin list.

Various agencies (including the FBI, Customs, Drug Enforcement Administration, IRS, Federal Reserve, and Treasury) are responsible for enforcing money laundering laws. FinCEN, a U.S. Treasury division, uses artificial intelligence technology to analyze all Currency Transaction Reports (CTRs), which persons must file with the U.S. government when they receive cash payments over $10,000, and Suspicious Activity Reports filed by banks, thrifts, credit unions, and commercial and law enforcement databases.

Various national, regional, and global agreements and institutions (such as the Inter-American Drug Abuse Control Commission of the Organization of American States) seek to combat money laundering. Financial Intelligence Units (FIUs), similar to Fin-CEN, have been formed in many countries to obtain and process financial disclosure information and support anti–money laundering efforts. The 1988 United Nations (UN) Drug Convention requires signatories to criminalize drug-related money laundering and to enact asset forfeiture laws.

> *"Launderers have devised an infinite number of schemes to hide the large sums that are generated by illicit drug sales."*

In 1989, the G-7 countries formed the Financial Action Task Force (FATF), which has issued 40 recommendations or standards to control money laundering. In 2000, the U.S. prompted the FATF to issue a report that identified 15 "non-cooperative countries and territories" (NCCTs) and stated that if they do not sufficiently comply within one year, they would be subject to countermeasures. In fact, almost immediately, the U.S. and other FATF members required financial institutions to increase scrutiny of transactions from NCCTs, thereby inhibiting or in some cases practically precluding most transactions from some of these jurisdictions. . . .

High Profits Overshadow Legal Consequences

Law enforcement, national security, and military agencies have lobbied vociferously and successfully for antinarcotics enforcement appropriations to offset reduced, post–cold war budgets. In May 1998, then President Clinton announced "a comprehensive international crime control strategy for America" in which he pledged to "seek new authority to fight money laundering and freeze the U.S. assets of people arrested abroad." Yet despite numerous laws, treaties, multilateral agreements, and public pronouncements, large-scale trafficking and money laundering continues, because the demand for drugs is high, profits are enormous, and detection is difficult. The average Colombian trafficking organization earns approximately $300 million annually, according to a 1994 State Department report.

The globalization of trade, finance, and communications has made it easier to transport illicit drugs, persons,

> *"Large-scale trafficking and money laundering continues, because the demand for drugs is high, profits are enormous, and detection is difficult."*

and commodities of all kinds and to launder the proceeds. Many criminals invest simultaneously in ships and planes in order to facilitate their trade in humans, drugs, art, automobiles, endangered species, and money. The sheer volume of financial transactions, many via wire transfers or electronic messages between banks, is staggering. Within the U.S., more than 465,000 wire transfers—valued at more than $2 trillion—are handled daily. Another 220,000 transfer messages are carried in and out of the United States by an international messaging system known as SWIFT (Society for Worldwide Interbank Financial Telecommunication). The large number of transactions precludes effective policing without sacrificing normal commerce.

In 1995, the Office of Technology Assessment (OTA) estimated that within the U.S. approximately 0.05% of transfers (or roughly 250 transactions a day) involve money laundering. Although a wire transfer initially contains information about the sender or originator of the transfer, as the transfer passes through several banks before reaching the beneficiary's account, the identification of the originator is often dropped. Under regulations issued in 1996, U.S. banks are required to identify the originator and the beneficiary of wire transfers, and such information must travel with the message throughout the transfer. But foreign banks are not required to supply this information.

Many Banking Options

Launderers utilize diverse services offered by international banks, financial institutions, and a host of intermediaries and professions. Private banks, correspondent banks, off-shore banks, internet banking and gaming, international business companies, international trusts, wire transfers, concentration accounts, automated teller machines, pass-through accounts, mortgages, and brokerage accounts provide a rich source of tools by which criminals and their agents can launder money.

> *"Launderers utilize diverse services offered by international banks, financial institutions, and a host of intermediaries and professions."*

OFCs—through which large sums of money are shifted from one country to another—involve intricate networks of accounts used to purchase homes, businesses, and investments with laundered funds. The Cayman Islands, for instance, is now the world's sixth largest financial center, according to investigative reporter Ken Silverstein. Concentration accounts permit funds from various individuals to be commingled without divulging their origins. Private banks, little known subdivisions of every major U.S. financial institution, offer regulatory deference to wealthy clients. For instance, Citibank established private banking services for Raul Salinas, brother of former Mexican President Carlos Salinas, without following its own internal rules on due diligence for starting such accounts. Raul Salinas then laundered tens of millions of dollars in drug money.

Although the U.S. is one of the leading money laundering centers, very few U.S. money laundering cases are actually prosecuted—an indication that this crime is difficult to detect and that inadequate resources are being devoted to enforcement. In 1995, only 62 criminal money laundering cases were filed with U.S. attorneys; of the 138 defendants, 52 were convicted.

Operation Casablanca

In May 1998, however, the Justice and Treasury departments announced the successful culmination of "Operation Casablanca," hailed as "the largest, most comprehensive drug money laundering case in the history of U.S. law enforcement." The three-year sting operation led to the arrest of 26 Mexican bank officials, the seizure of an estimated $150 million, and the freezing of over 100 bank accounts in the United States and Europe.

The case resulted in fierce diplomatic protests by Mexico, because the U.S. violated its sovereignty by conducting undercover operations in Mexican territory without Mexico's knowledge, approval, or participation, as required by various international and bilateral agreements. In April 2001, however, the Mexican government of Vicente Fox shifted course and signaled its willingness to allow U.S. intelligence and law enforcement officials unprecedented access to share intelligence.

The detection of money laundering is impeded by various national and international laws that protect individual rights to financial, communication, and data privacy. In the United States, the Right to Financial Privacy Act of 1978 provides many of the procedural protections for financial records guaranteed more broadly by the Fourth Amendment. The Electronic Communications Privacy Act of 1986 essentially prohibits the monitoring of wire transfers while in transit or in storage without a court order, warrant, or administrative subpoena.

In a significant number of countries, bank secrecy laws buffer the release of comprehensive data about financial transactions by prohibiting banking officials from divulging customer information to persons outside the financial institution or by blocking access by foreign law enforcement agencies on the grounds of national sovereignty. Additionally, under data protection laws such as the European Union's (EU) Data Protection Directive, information may be prohibited from leaving a signatory country if it is being sent to a country with less stringent data protection laws. The EU privacy rights require that records of suspicious transactions and intelligence information be destroyed after a period of years, unless prosecutors have taken enforcement action; the U.S. policy is to keep such information indefinitely. . . .

Toward a New Foreign Policy

Although various international standards have been written to guide governments in adopting anti-money laundering policies, not all jurisdictions have implemented regulations. "Soft law" standards, in the form of recommendations, should be transformed into hard law through international conventions with effective enforcement provisions.

Regulations and procedures for banks and other financial institutions need to be evenhanded and in close conformity with those of other countries. Washington should reconsider the advisability of unilateral extraterritorial sanctions and operations, unless the U.S. has exhausted all means of cooperative approaches to kingpin and related sanctions. The Bush administration should, for instance, respond to the Vicente Fox government's new openness in sharing intelligence not by unilaterally operating inside Mexico but by building collaborative procedures for detecting and prosecuting international money laundering, corruption, and drug trafficking. And the White House should follow the recommendations of the congressionally created Judicial Re-

"The detection of money laundering is impeded by various national and international laws that protect individual [privacy] rights."

94

view Commission on Foreign Asset Control, whose January 2001 report, based on the Foreign Narcotics Kingpin Designation Act (Kingpin Act), recommended that the Office of Foreign Asset Control (OFAC) adopt greater openness and responsiveness and submit to more formal administrative review of its final actions.

> *"The illicit drug trade funds powerful criminal organizations, resulting in widespread corruption, violence, and an undermining of the rule of law."*

Washington should realize the limitations of harsh enforcement policies, such as anti–money laundering measures and economic sanctions, on illicit drug trafficking. These regulations can only have a minor effect on curtailing money laundering. In 1995, the OTA found that anti–money laundering regulations do not work, because the number of money laundering transactions is believed to be relatively small, insufficient information is contained in wire transfers, and it is difficult to characterize a typical money laundering transaction, rendering identification and profiling very problematic. In addition, a tougher system would, as noted by the Judicial Review Commission, also pose a serious threat to privacy and constitutional protections.

The illicit drug trade funds powerful criminal organizations, resulting in widespread corruption, violence, and an undermining of the rule of law. This, in turn, impedes the prosecution of these organizations, weakens the judicial system, and prevents the effective implementation of anti–money laundering controls in the banking system. Weak legal structures and social instability also thwart legal commercial development. The allocation of enforcement resources to combat international drug money laundering and drug trafficking is disproportionate to the harm from the trade and restricts the ability of law enforcement bodies to focus on violent forms of crime, such as terrorism, weapons trafficking, and trafficking in human beings.

Combat the Demand for Drugs

Rather than simply increasing the enforcement regime against money laundering and drug trafficking, greater emphasis should be placed on actions and resources that address the fundamental causes of the problem—namely, the demand for drugs and the lack of economic opportunities in both developing countries and U.S. urban centers. In the U.S., more emphasis should be placed on addiction treatment and urban development in an effort to curb drug demand and sales. This would, in turn, reduce the proceeds to drug traffickers. Although drug trafficking and money laundering will be reduced if the demand for illicit drugs is reduced in consumer countries and if alternative forms of development are implemented in source and transit countries, drug consumption will continue to exist. The artificially high profits from supplying drug consumers serve to impede alternative forms of development.

Ultimately, the UN Conventions on Illicit Drugs (1961, 1971, 1988) must be revised to allow for signatory parties to experiment in regulating the distribution and sale of certain illicit drugs. Unfortunately, . . . actions by the UN make it clear that such experiments will not be considered. A UN counterdrug plan proposed to the 1998 General Assembly Special Session on Illicit Drugs is useful in promoting crop substitution programs, but it sets the wholly unrealistic goal of eradicating the world's entire production of heroin, cocaine, and marijuana by the year 2008.

There are a variety of regulation schemes that could be implemented to control access to drugs while removing the profits from criminal enterprises. Ideally, the aim should be to minimize the harm that drugs cause to users and society at large, to shrink the size of the black market, and to obviate the need to launder illicit funds.

Drug Trafficking Has Corrupted the American Government

by Gary Webb

About the author: *In 1996, Gary Webb wrote a controversial three-part newspaper series exposing the CIA's alleged involvement in drug trafficking. He has since written a book titled* Dark Alliance: The CIA, the Contras, and the Crack Cocaine Explosion *(Seven Stories Press), and currently serves as a consultant to the California State Legislature Task Force on Government Oversight.*

For the record, let me just say this right now. I do not believe—and I have never believed—that the crack cocaine explosion was a conscious CIA conspiracy, or anybody's conspiracy, to decimate black America. I've never believed that South Central Los Angeles was targeted by the U.S. government to become the crack capital of the world. But that isn't to say that the CIA's hands or the U.S. government's hands are clean in this matter. Actually, far from it. After spending three years of my life looking into this, I am more convinced than ever that the U.S. government's responsibility for the drug problems in South Central Los Angeles and other inner cities is greater than I ever wrote in the newspaper.

But it's important to differentiate between malign intent and gross negligence. And that's an important distinction, because it's what makes premeditated murder different from manslaughter. That said, it doesn't change the fact that you've got a body on the floor, and that's what I want to talk about, the body....

What I've attempted to demonstrate in my book *Dark Alliance*, was how the collapse of a brutal, pro-American dictatorship in Latin America, combined with a decision by corrupt CIA agents to raise money for a resistance movement by any means necessary, led to the formation of the nation's first major crack market in South Central Los Angeles, which led to the arming and the empowerment of LA's street gangs, which led to the spread of crack to black

Excerpted from "CIA Connections to Contra Drug Trafficking," speech by Gary Webb, January 16, 1999, Eugene, Oregon, while on tour promoting his book *Dark Alliance*. Reprinted with the author's permission.

neighborhoods across the country, and to the passage of racially discriminatory sentencing laws that are locking up thousands of young black men today behind bars for most of their lives.

But it's not so much a conspiracy as a chain reaction. And that's what my whole book is about, this chain reaction. So let me explain the links in this chain a little better.

Revolution in Nicaragua

The first link is this fellow Anastasio Somoza, who was an American-educated tyrant, one of our buddies naturally, and his family ruled Nicaragua for forty years—thanks to the Nicaraguan National Guard, which we supplied, armed, and funded, because we thought they were anti-communists.

In 1979, the people of Nicaragua got tired of living under this dictatorship, and they rose up and overthrew it. And a lot of Somoza's friends and relatives and business partners came to the United States, because we had been their allies all these years, including two men, Danilo Blandón and Norwin Meneses, whose families had been very close to the dictatorship. . . .

They came to the United States in 1979, along with a flood of other Nicaraguan immigrants, most of them middle-class people, most of them former bankers, former insurance salesmen—sort of a capitalist exodus from Nicaragua. And they got involved when they got here, and they decided they were going to take the country back; they didn't like the fact that they'd been forced out of their country. So they formed these resistance organizations here in the United States, and they began plotting how they were going to kick the Sandanistas [rebels] out. . . .

The CIA Gets Involved

In 1979 and 1980, the CIA secretly began visiting these groups that were setting up here in the United States, supplying them with a little bit of money, and telling them to hold on, wait for a little while, don't give up. And Ronald Reagan came to town. Reagan saw what happened in Nicaragua not as a populist uprising, as most of the rest of the world did. He saw it as this band of communists down there. . . . Which fit in very well with the CIA's thinking. So, the CIA under Reagan got it together, and they said, "We're going to help these guys out." They authorized $19 million to fund a covert war to destabilize the government in Nicaragua and help get their old buddies back in power.

> *"I am more convinced than ever that the U.S. government's responsibility for the drug problems . . . is greater than I ever wrote in the newspaper."*

Soon after the CIA took over this operation, these two drug traffickers, who had come from Nicaragua and settled in California, were called down to Honduras. And they met with a CIA agent named Enrique Bermúdez, who was one of Somoza's military officials, and the man the CIA picked to run this new organization they were forming. And both traffickers had said—one of them said, the other one wrote, and it's never been contradicted—that when they met with the CIA agent, he told them, "We need money for this operation. Your guy's job is to go to California and raise money, and not to worry about how you did it. And what he said was—and I think this had been used to justify just about every crime against humanity that we've known—"the ends justify the means.". . . .

Sometime in 1982, Danilo Blandón, who had been given the Los Angeles market, started selling his cocaine to a young drug dealer named Ricky Ross, who later became known as "Freeway" Rick. In 1994, the *Los Angeles Times* would describe him as the master marketer most responsible for flooding the streets of Los Angeles with cocaine. . . .

He lived in South Central Los Angeles, which was home to some street gangs known as the Crips and the Bloods. And back in 1981–82, hardly anybody knew who they were. They were mainly neighborhood kids—they'd beat each other up, they'd steal leather coats, they'd steal cars, but they were really nothing back then. But what they gained through this organization, and what they gained through Ricky Ross, was a built-in distribution network throughout the neighborhood. The Crips and the Bloods were already selling marijuana, they were already selling PCP, so it wasn't much of a stretch for them to sell something new, which is what these Nicaraguans were bringing in, which was cocaine. . . .

> *"[Reagan] saw [Nicaragua] as this band of communists down there."*

The Emergence of Crack

So by the time crack got ahold of South Central, which took a couple of years, Rick had positioned himself on top of the crack market. And by 1984, crack sales had supplanted marijuana and PCP sales as sources of income for the gangs and drug dealers of South Central. And suddenly these guys had more money than they knew what to do with. Because what happened with crack, it democratized the drug. When you were buying it in powdered form, you were having to lay out a hundred bucks for a gram, or a hundred and fifty bucks for a gram. Now all you needed was ten bucks, or five bucks, or a dollar—they were selling "dollar rocks" at one point. So anybody who had money and wanted to get high could get some of this stuff. You didn't need to be a middle-class or wealthy drug user anymore. . . .

By 1985, the LA crack market had become saturated. There was so much dope going into South Central, dope that the CIA, we now know, knew of, and they knew the origins of—the FBI knew the origins of it; the DEA knew the origins of it; and nobody did anything about it. . . .

Today, fortunately, crack use is on a downward trend, but that's something that isn't due to any great progress we've made in the so-called "War on Drugs," it's the natural cycle of things. Drug epidemics generally run from 10 to 15 years. Heroin is now the latest drug on the upswing.

Now, a lot of people disagreed with this scenario. *The New York Times*, the *Los Angeles Times* and the *Washington Post* all came out and said, oh, no, that's not so. They said this couldn't have happened that way, be-

> *"By 1984, crack sales had supplanted marijuana and PCP sales as sources of income for the gangs and drug dealers of South Central."*

cause crack would have happened anyway. Which is true, somewhat. As I pointed out in the first chapter of my book, crack was on its way here. But whether it would have happened the same way, whether it would have happened in South Central, whether it would have happened in Los Angeles at all first, is a very different story. If it had happened in Eugene, Oregon first, it might not have gone anywhere. No offense, but those folks aren't exactly trend setters when it comes to drug dealers and drug fads. LA is, however.

You can play "what if" games all you like, but it doesn't change the reality. And the reality is that this CIA-connected drug ring played a very critical role in the early 1980s in opening up South Central to a crack epidemic that was unmatched in its severity and influence anywhere in the U.S. . . . .

The Media's Contribution

One of the things which these newspapers who dissed my story were saying was, we can't believe that the CIA would know about drug trafficking and let it happen. That this idea that this agency which gets $27 billion a year to tell us what's going on, and which was so intimately involved with the contras they were writing their press releases for them, they wouldn't know about this drug trafficking going on under their noses. But the *Los Angeles Times* and the *Washington Post* all uncritically reported their claims that the CIA didn't know what was going on, and that it would never permit its hirelings to do anything like that, as unseemly as drug trafficking. You know, assassinations and bombings and that sort of thing, yeah, they'll admit to right up front, but drug dealing, no, no, they don't do that kind of stuff.

Unfortunately, though, it was true, and what has happened since my series came out is that the CIA was forced to do an internal review, the DEA and Justice Department were forced to do internal reviews, and these agencies that released these reports, you probably didn't read about them, because they contradicted everything else these other newspapers had been writing for the last couple of years, but let me just read you this one excerpt. This is from a 1987 DEA report. And this is about this drug ring in Los Angeles that I wrote about. In 1987, the DEA sent undercover informants inside this drug operation, and they interviewed one of the principals of this organization, namely Ivan Torres. And this is what he said. He told the informant:

"The CIA wants to know about drug trafficking, but only for their own purposes, and not necessarily for the use of law enforcement agencies. Torres told a DEA Confidential Informant that CIA representatives are aware of his drug-related activities, and that they don't mind. He said they had gone so far as to encourage cocaine trafficking by members of the contras, because they know it's a good source of income. Some of this money has gone into numbered accounts in Europe and Panama, as does the money that goes to Managua from cocaine trafficking. Torres told the informant about receiving counterintelligence training from the CIA, and had avowed that the CIA looks the other way and in essence allows them to engage in narcotics trafficking.". . .

So, the one thing that I've learned from this whole experience is, first of all, you can't believe the government—on anything. And you especially can't believe them when they're talking about important stuff, like this stuff. The other thing is that the media will believe the government before they believe anything. . . .

A Pivotal Agreement

Something came out just recently, which nobody seems to know about, because it hasn't been reported—the CIA Inspector General went before Congress in March 1998 and testified that yes, they knew about it. They found some documents that indicated that they knew about it. . . .

One of the people said, "well geez, what was the CIA's responsibility when they found out about this? What were you guys supposed to do?" And the Inspector General sort of looked around nervously, cleared his throat and said, "Well . . . that's kind of an odd history there." And [reporter] Norman Dix from Washington didn't let it go at that. He said, "Explain what you mean by that?" And the Inspector General said, "well, we were looking around and we found this document, and according to the document, we didn't have to report this to anybody." And they said, "How come?" And the Inspector General said, "we don't know exactly, but there was an agreement made in 1982 . . . that said if there is drug trafficking involved by CIA agents, we don't have to tell the Justice Department." Actually, this is now a public record, this document. . . .

> *"Today, fortunately, crack use is on a downward trend."*

So I think that eliminates any questions that drug trafficking by the contras was an accident, or was a matter of just a few rotten apples. I think what this said was that it was anticipated by the Justice Department, it was anticipated by the CIA, and steps were taken to ensure that there was a loophole in the law, so that if it ever became public knowledge, nobody would be prosecuted for it. . . .

[This is] one thing that we can do, [and that] is [to] force the House Intelligence Committee to hold hearings on this. This is supposed to be the oversight committee of the CIA. They have held one hearing, and after they found out there was this deal that they didn't have to report drug trafficking, they all ran out of the room, they haven't convened since.

So if you're interested in pursuing this, the thing I would suggest you do is, call up the House Intelligence Committee in Washington and ask them when we're going to have another CIA/contra/crack hearing. Believe me, it'll drive them crazy. Send them email, just ask them, make sure—they think everybody's forgotten about this. . . . I don't think it's been forgotten. They want us to forget about it. They want us to concentrate on sex crimes, because, yeah, it's titillating. It keeps us occupied. It keeps us diverted. Don't let them do it.

Drug Trafficking Has Corrupted the Mexican Government

by Terrence Poppa

About the author: *Terrence Poppa, a former reporter, is the author of* Drug Lord: The Life and Death of a Mexican Kingpin, *an exposé of how drug trafficking is organized in Mexico.*

To read the newspapers, it would seem that Mexico finally is getting its act together in the drug war. On May 4, 2000, dozens of Mexican federal police and soldiers arrested the second in command of the Arellano Felix [drug cartel] after a shootout in Baja California. Mexico's top prosecutor trumpeted the importance of the arrest in a news conference: "This criminal organization has been put on the run. We are dismantling them," he said.

The Arellano Felix brothers, the notoriously violent crime lords of Tijuana, indeed may be on the run and ultimately may be arrested or killed. As desirable as that would be, Mexico's actions against them had nothing to do with law enforcement. They had only to do with the control and regulation of a lucrative criminal activity that the government of Mexico itself sponsored. What Americans have difficulty understanding about Mexico, and the relationship between Mexico and the drug plague in the United States, is that the Mexican government has been deliberately involved in drug trafficking for decades, using the federal police agencies and the military to pump vast amounts of narcotics into the United States. The Mexican government franchises drug trafficking and controls the franchises along the administrative lines established by the government for its federal police agencies and the military. Someone is given control of the plaza—essentially an administrative area—in exchange for a "quota"—the protection fee based on the total volume of activity. For decades Mexican informants tried to explain the idea to their law-enforcement contacts in the United States. When somebody has the plaza, it means that he

Reprinted from "Q: Is the Mexican Government Fueling America's Drug Plague? Yes: Top Mexican Officials Sanction, Control, and Profit from the Drug Trade and Have for Years," by Terrence Poppa, Symposium feature in *Insight*, June 12, 2000, p. 40. Copyright 2000 News World Communications, Inc. All rights reserved. Reprinted with permission of *Insight*.

is paying an authority or authorities with sufficient power to ensure that he will not be bothered by state or federal police or by the military. The protection money goes up the ladder, with percentages shaved off at each level up the chain of command until reaching the Grand Protector or the Grand Protectors in the scheme.

The Plaza Holder

To stay in the good graces of his patrons in power, the plaza holder has a dual obligation: to generate money for his protectors and to lend his intelligence-gathering abilities by fingering the independent operators—those narcotics traffickers and drug growers who try to avoid paying the necessary tribute. The independents are the ones who get busted by the Mexican Federal Judicial Police, the Mexican equivalent of the FBI, or by the army, providing Mexico with statistics to show it is involved in authentic drug enforcement.

True, drug seizures in fact are made, and headlines and photos prove it. Most of the seized narcotics then are recycled—sold to favored trafficking groups or outrightly smuggled by police groups. Usually, the authorities protect the plaza holder from rival drug lords; in some cases they hold back and allow the bloody process of natural selection to determine who shall run the plaza. If the authorities arrest or kill the plaza holder, it usually is because he has stopped making payments or because his name has started to appear in the press too frequently and the trafficker has become a liability. Sometimes international pressure gets so strong that the government is forced to take action against a specific individual—regardless of how much money he is generating for the system.

This was the fate of the Arellano Felix brothers. Though they once had operated under an umbrella of protection, they fell out of favor following the murder of a Roman Catholic cardinal at the airport in Guadalajara in 1994—allegedly gunned down by hit men of the Arellano Felix faction in an ambush intended for a rival group. The brothers have not wanted to go quietly. They and the government of Mexico have been at war ever since, with government forces to date suffering more losses than the outlaw drug faction.

From the Top Down

In Mexico crime groups do not buy and intimidate their way in and up the ladder of officialdom. This may happen in border towns governed by opposition parties that refuse to be a part of the corrupt federal system. In general, however, the federal system corrupts downwardly, recruiting crime elements into the system to further the government's own vast crime activities, using individual criminals and their organizations as front men and fall guys.

This can be seen in the way federal police commanders are assigned to their offices. The federal comandantes, many of whom have underworld origins, typically buy their positions from the attorney general's office. Comandantes pay varying amounts for control of a particular plaza—$1 million for a position in the interior of Mexico, $2 million for a coastal plaza and $3 million for a border plaza. The comandantes then pay a monthly quota to their bosses, money collected not only from protected drug-trafficking organizations but also from auto-theft rings that steal automobiles by the thousands from the United States and from organizations that smuggle illegal immigrants. My interviews with the people directly involved with cross-border drug shipments proved beyond any doubt that the government of Mexico always is in charge.

Witness the following story by a former drug pilot and right-hand man of Juan Garcia Abrego, the now jailed former drug lord of Matamoros. In the late seventies, the pilot frequently would fly south to Oaxaca to pick up marijuana loads from a camp run by the Directorate of Federal Security, the Interior government secret police. On occasions when walking from his airplane to the encampment, he would see human heads sticking out of the ground. He did not know if these people were dead or alive, but he understood that their presence was a warning to anyone coming into the camp: Play by our rules or it will be your head sticking out of the ground. It is the government of Mexico that is in control of the drug traffickers, not the other way around.

Government as a Business

Americans need to understand that the involvement of the Mexican political system in drug trafficking is a symptom of the nature of the Mexican political system, of the Institutional Revolutionary Party system—the PRI—that has ruled Mexico for seven decades. In Mexico, government is a business. It is a money-making machine for the people that run it. The more power, the more money that can be made. Involvement in organized crime is only one of the ways to make money. The more traditional road to self enrichment is stealing public money through one embezzlement scheme or another.

One only needs to examine examples of "corruption" to grasp the magnitude of this: Recall Raul Salinas de Gortari, the brother of former Mexican president Carlos Salinas de Gortari. During his brother's tenure, Raul made a fortune from his government post as director of Mexico's food-subsidy program and also through protection that he was providing Juan Garcia Abrego, the Matamoros cocaine kingpin. Salinas was known as "Mr. Ten Percent" for the kickbacks he demanded for all food subsidy program contracts. The Salinas family's involvement in these kinds of criminal activities never

"The Mexican government has been deliberately involved in drug trafficking for decades."

would have been exposed if Raul Salinas had not gotten involved in high-profile killings. He later was arrested and convicted for the murder of Jose Francisco Ruiz Massieu, his ex-brother-in-law and a former president of the PRI party, who was assassinated in 1994. Swiss and British authorities seized some $120 million in Raul Salinas' secret deposits, but a Swiss investigation later estimated conservatively that Raul Salinas made a half-billion dollars from protection for drug trafficking while Carlos Salinas was president. Can anyone truly believe that Carlos was not a part of this?

The Raul Salinas example is only that—a mere example. The theft of public money in Mexico is routine and affects every federal and state agency in the hands of the PRI. It bleeds Mexico systematically of the tax monies generated by the private sector. Such money in a normal country goes into building roads and bridges, schools, public transit and public enterprises, assuring steady growth of businesses both large and small. In Mexico, however, much of that money goes into private pockets or secret accounts in offshore banks, leaving schools unstaffed and roads unbuilt. It may be argued that the root cause of Mexico's stagnant economy is the systematic looting of the public treasury by robber bureaucrats.

> *"The federal system corrupts downwardly, recruiting crime elements into the system to further the government's own vast crime activities."*

Corrupt Presidents

The involvement in drugs has included every president of Mexico and his chief cabinet members since at least the 1970s. As a rule, people become president of Mexico because they are willing to represent the interests of the narcopolitical complex of which they are already a part. If they were unwilling or unable to represent these interests, they would not become president. They do not go into office high-minded and then succumb to temptation. They go into office fully expecting and intending to become immensely wealthy during their six-year reign. A hint of the truth of this came through the Casa Blanca investigation, a U.S. Customs money-laundering sting in 1998 in Mexico which led to the arrest of more than 100 Mexican bankers lured to Las Vegas after the evidence in Mexico had been gathered on them. One of the bankers targeted by the sting came forward with an offer to launder $1.15 billion in drug money belonging to President Ernesto Zedillo, Zedillo's defense minister and other cabinet members. The Bill Clinton administration dropped the investigation at that point, refusing to pursue this promising lead into the heart of Mexico's political darkness. It is fair, therefore, for Americans to draw their own conclusions.

The deliberate protection mechanisms for organized crime have enriched Mexico's ruling class and turned drug trafficking in Mexico into a national industry. Like a parting of the Red Sea, this has assured safe passage through Mexico to the United States of ever-increasing volumes of hard drugs. In 2000, 2 million Americans were in jail, twice the number since 1990, and the majority were behind bars for drug-related crimes. Even so, American drug agencies estimate that there are still 4 million hard-core drug users—people who are chemically enslaved—in the United States.

These numbers will continue to escalate as long as the drug supply continues to escalate. The deliberate and organized protection for drug trafficking by the government of Mexico is a mechanism that, unless it is recognized for what it is and dealt with in a forthright manner, will result in the continuing and ever-accelerating degradation of American life and of American institutions.

Chapter 3

Can International Assistance to Colombia Combat Drug Trafficking?

CURRENT CONTROVERSIES

Chapter Preface

In 1948, the Liberal Party candidate for the Colombian presidency was assassinated, initiating a nine-year period of terror known as La Violencia. Although La Violencia officially ended with a compromising pact called the National Front in 1957, Marxist forces such as the Revolutionary Armed Forces of Colombia (know by the Spanish acronym FARC) and the National Liberation Army (ELN) have violently struggled against military and right-wing paramilitary forces for a larger share of political power for more than forty years.

Many argue that providing assistance to Colombia's antidrug efforts entangles the United States in their civil war. They argue that most of the aid sent to the Colombian military is used to fight the rebels rather than the battle against drug trafficking. Despite atrocities committed by both the paramilitaries and the guerrillas, supporters claim that the United States funds operations that target the Communist rebels and ignores similar actions by the paramilitaries. According to freelance journalist Frank Smyth, "[The CIA] maintain[s] warm relationships with rightist military forces . . . that are engaging in widespread human-rights abuses. These ties conflict with the agency's putative goal of fighting drugs, since many of the rightist allies are themselves involved in the drug trade."

Others maintain that the flow of drugs into the United States cannot be halted unless Colombia receives assistance to fight both the drug war and their civil war. As both sides are funded by drug traffickers, the insurgent guerrillas and the Colombian military are characterized by corruption and violence. According to Francis Fukuyama, professor of public policy at George Mason University, "The biggest questions today are whether the Colombian military . . . can be turned around with better training and equipment. We won't know until we try." Fukuyama and others contend that the war against drug trafficking cannot be won without also assisting the Colombian government in regaining control of the paramilitary forces and the parts of the country ruled by the insurgent guerrillas.

The U.S. involvement in Colombia's civil war is one of the issues discussed in the following chapter on whether Colombia should receive international assistance to restore order and fight drug trafficking.

U.S. Assistance May Combat Drug Trafficking in Colombia

by Rafael Pardo

About the author: *Rafael Pardo was a special adviser for peace negotiations to the president of Colombia from 1986 to 1990 and Colombia's first civilian minister of defense from 1991 to 1994.*

During the 1980s, Latin America was at the forefront of U.S. foreign and security policy. But as the Cold War ended and local conflicts subsided, the region slipped onto a strategic back burner. Washington's interest in it was sparked chiefly by financial opportunities or crises. Now Latin American battles are once again in the news as civil strife in Colombia becomes a serious security threat not only to the Andean region but to the broader hemisphere as well.

The Colombian conflict is deep-rooted and complex, involving two basic issues (drugs and control of the country) and three warring factions (the government, left-wing guerrillas, and right-wing paramilitaries). What is more, it is now boiling over: in addition to battling the government, the guerrillas kidnap neighboring Venezuelans and Ecuadorians; the paramilitaries smuggle weapons from bases along the Panamanian border; and hundreds of citizens from dozens of foreign countries are taken hostage annually. Despite years of antidrug efforts and the destruction of the powerful Medellín and Cali drug cartels, Colombia remains the world's largest producer and exporter of cocaine and the second-largest supplier of heroin to the United States.

These problems cannot be solved by Colombians alone. The country needs international help, particularly American engagement. But foreign involvement will make a difference only if it comes in the proper form.

The Clinton administration proposed a $1.7 billion aid package, the largest in Colombian history. Of this, $1 billion would go toward improving the Colombian military's capacity to suppress coca planting—buying helicopters, spare

From "Colombia's Two-Front War," by Rafael Pardo. Reprinted by permission of *Foreign Affairs*, July/August 2000. Copyright 2000 by the Council on Foreign Relations, Inc.

parts, training, and intelligence equipment to help the army destroy coca crops and retake guerrilla-held areas. The other $700 million would finance coca substitution programs, public works in sensitive regions, and improvements in Colombia's judicial system and human rights protections. The U.S. aid would be part of a broader three-year, $7 billion "Plan Colombia" that includes multilateral loans and contributions from Europe. The plan is designed to strengthen Colombian institutions, sponsor regional development of the coca areas, and help reduce drug production.

Plan Colombia is an important step in the right direction, and most ordinary citizens have welcomed it. We Colombians understand that the drug issue is critical, not least because the guerrillas and paramilitary forces rely on the financial backing of drug traffickers to keep fighting. But we also know that the conflict involves more than drugs and that, by itself, Plan Colombia will not answer all our problems.

Those problems are not to be taken lightly. The cost of the drug war has been staggering. In the last 15 years, 200 bombs (half of them as large as the one used in Oklahoma City in 1995) have blown up in Colombia's cities; an entire democratic leftist political party was eliminated by right-wing paramilitaries; 4 presidential candidates, 200 judges and investigators, half the Supreme Court's justices, 1,200 police officers, 151 journalists, and more than 300,000 ordinary Colombians have been murdered.

Despite this toll, the international community in general and the United States in particular must understand that the Colombian government's conflict with the guerrillas can be solved only through negotiations. If the current peace talks fail, the country will plunge into all-out war and Colombians will lose their democracy. Early in the negotiations, the United States met privately with the main rebel group, the Revolutionary Armed Forces of Colombia ([known by the Spanish acronym] FARC), but American participation was suspended after FARC killed three human rights activists. The guerrillas have shown little remorse and exonerated the commanders who the American and Colombian police believe ordered the killings. But making sure the peace process moves forward is so important that the United States should get substantively involved once again and make a negotiated end to the war in Colombia a central goal of American foreign policy.

The Coca Lords

The roots of Colombia's current drug problems lie in the decision by local smugglers and traffickers to turn the traditional Andean coca crop into a thriving international business. In 1975, these entrepreneurs were already producing 70 percent of the world's supply of marijuana. Looking ahead, they saw better prospects in cocaine. (Two decades later, in much the same way, they would capitalize on growth opportunities in heroin.) In the 1970s, cocaine was available in the United States and Europe, but it was expensive and hard to find.

Colombian drug interests financed experiments until they hit on a formula for coca paste: crushed coca leaves mixed with gasoline, cement, and ether. This recipe produced cocaine chlorohydrate, which was then dried in the middle of the jungle in ordinary microwave ovens operated by generators. The resulting cocaine was shipped to U.S. markets in small planes and sold for up to $30,000 per kilogram in New York and Chicago.

The keys to the scheme's success were that the formula was simple and the ingredients were readily available. The new method made the traffickers much richer and gave rise to the drug cartels, which came to specialize in particular niches of the drug economy: transportation, processing, money laundering, and distribution. When the cartels realized that regular, powder cocaine was too expensive to market in poor communities, the drug lords then invented "crack," and another stage in the business—and the world's addictive nightmare—was born.

The growth of the cartels turned Colombia upside down. In 1978, Colombia's drug revenue was $2 billion. By 1985, that flow had increased to $3 billion—an astronomical figure, given that Colombia's gross national product was then only $40 billion. The wealth was grabbed by a few hands and invested in such safe sectors as urban real estate and huge rural haciendas. (This helped create the coalition between landowners and drug traffickers that now finances the paramilitaries.) Drug prices shot up, and the flow of dollars multiplied, throwing off the exchange rate. Traffickers used their dollars to buy lux-

"[Colombia] needs international help, particularly American engagement."

ury items and other merchandise abroad and sell them for less than their value at the duty-free zones that sprang up around Colombia. Today, for example, one can buy a Japanese stereo in Colombia for less than in Tokyo. Such unfair competition almost destroyed the legitimate local Colombian economy.

The booming cocaine industry also deformed Colombia's morals. Riches, no matter how ill-gotten, became the goal of many Colombians, and respect for civic rights, education, and honest work declined. The judicial system and other government institutions crumbled before narcotraffickers determined to carve out a sphere for their illicit businesses through violence and corruption.

Government Efforts

The Colombian state tried to deal with these problems but was simply too weak. In 1979, for example, Colombia and the United States signed an extradition treaty that would permit Colombian nationals to be tried in the United States. Such treaties are hardly unusual, but in Colombia the deal elicited a declaration of war from its likely targets. With their fortunes, the drug traffickers organized an armed gang called the Extraditables and launched a terrorist campaign with the motto, "We prefer a tomb in Colombia to a jail cell in the United States." To show it meant business, the group assassinated a

Colombian Supreme Court justice. The war then moved on to journalists, politicians, and police officers. Hit men received $2,000 for each cop they killed. Eventually the drug lords went after Colombia's civil society as well. They blew up a plane with 109 passengers on board, set off car bombs in shopping malls, and dynamited the headquarters of the federal investigative agency. They even financed the passage of a constitutional amendment by the Colombian Congress prohibiting extradition.

Lawlessness spread uncontrollably not because of a lack of controls or laws but because the combination of drugs, corruption, and insurgency makes any type of control ludicrous. Colombia has one of the most sophisticated legal systems in the hemisphere and every conceivable law in the book, but 70 percent of all crimes remain unsolved, and it ranks among the top three most corrupt countries in the world according to Transparency International.

In September 1989, the Bush administration declared a new war on drugs, granting more aid and coordinating a multilateral approach with other Andean countries. But Colom-

> *"The keys to the scheme's success were that the formula was simple and the ingredients were readily available."*

bia was tired of the fight, beaten down by violence. Within a year, a constituent assembly elected by popular vote prohibited extradition, taking the heat off the drug kingpins. The government introduced a plea-bargaining policy that led to the partial dismantling of the cartels and the arrest of some key drug figures. But thanks to the weakness of the prison system, the cartel leaders continued to operate from behind bars. In 1992, the leader of the Medellín cartel, Pablo Escobar, escaped, and terrorism was unleashed again. But the government's military and judicial capacity had improved over the years, and Colombian police were able to gun down Escobar and finish off the Medellín cartel by the end of 1993.

Although the government has been doing somewhat better recently, even if it conquers its present troubles Colombia will always have a big problem in its midst. The country has eliminated the drug cartels, but it has never understood that the drug trade from the 1970s and 1980s created a new social class—an elite that grew rich through drug trafficking, that will fight to keep its business alive and thriving, and that is quite willing to use violence, terrorism, and corruption. Such people financed the guerrillas and paramilitaries. The drug class has spread corruption money around Congress and other Colombian institutions and financed the campaign of a former president. Traffickers know their market, and they knew that they should not work in big cartels. That business acumen has paid off, and more cocaine than ever is now being imported to the United States, according to recent reports. The violence produced by traffickers in Colombia is closely linked to the appetite of consumers in the United States and Europe—another good reason why attention must be paid.

Guerrillas in the Mist

In a parallel set of developments, Colombia became embroiled in a local variant of the Cold War during the 1960s. Rural guerrillas gained influence in the country's jungles and mountains. The armed bands were made up of the remnants of peasant groups that had rebelled against the government in the previous decade (later gathered into FARC) and newer groups promoted by Cuba (including the National Liberation Army, or ELN). These guerrillas caused some harm but never threatened the country's stability.

That began to change in the 1970s, when new urban terrorist groups started to appear. The best known of these, the M-19, burst onto the scene in 1982 when it took over the Dominican Republic's embassy in Bogotá. The group held 14 senior diplomats hostage, including the papal nuncio and the U.S. ambassador; after negotiations, they left for Cuba with some of the hostages and $5 million. The M-19 followed up this coup with other spectacular stunts, including a dramatic 1985 takeover of the Palace of Justice, during which they kidnapped the entire Colombian Supreme Court and exchanged heavy fire with the Colombian army. In the end, more than 100 people were left dead, including most of the justices.

In 1989, the government began serious peace talks with the M-19 that culminated in a peace accord the following year. Several smaller guerrilla groups also took part, and some 5,000 rebels wound up turning in their weapons. As part of the deal, the government designated temporary demilitarized zones in the countryside where the demobilized rebel troops would be safe from outside harassment to give them a measure of security during the negotiations. The settlement worked, and today many of these former guerrillas are prominent politicians and public officials.

But the two largest guerrilla forces—FARC, which has 12,000–15,000 troops, and the ELN, which has 3,000–5,000—refused to demobilize. Both groups had found independent financing that let them remain in the field and even grow stronger over time. The ELN, a Marxist/Christian group led until 1998 by a Spanish Catholic priest, discovered a profitable niche extorting money from oil companies. Since 1985, the group has bombed Colombia's main pipeline about 700 times—every week or so, that is—wasting 1.7 million barrels of oil and causing serious environmental damage.

Land Power

Meanwhile, FARC built up a presence in coca-growing areas, where it charged fees to plantations for "protection." In the mid-1990s, a disease destroyed almost 30 percent of the coca plantations in Peru's upper Huallaga Valley. Drug traffickers shifted their crops to Colombia's jungles, experimenting with the plants and producing a stronger coca leaf with a higher cocaine yield. As a result, the area of Colombia used for coca cultivation jumped from 20,000 to 120,000 hectares in five years. FARC took control of the crops and boosted its income to more than $600 million a year, making it possibly the richest insurgent group in history.

The coca plantations also provided the guerrillas with a social base for the first time in their 30 years of existence. This became visible in 1996, when coca growers held mass protests against a crop eradication push by the army. (In Colombia, most growers are not peasants—as they are in Peru and Bolivia—but hired hands recruited by traffickers from elsewhere in the country.) Egged on by FARC, more than 100,000 of these workers marched for several weeks. To end the uprising, the government agreed to limit its fumigation program to coca plantations smaller than three hectares.

Weak government institutions and guerrilla abuses opened a space for the emergence of various paramilitary forces. These groups are not formally linked with the Colombian army but often maintain some ties with it at the field level. Over the last five years, the paramilitaries have developed a common antiguerrilla political rhetoric and a centralized operational command. They are responsible for most of the country's human rights violations, including the assassinations of thousands of peasants. Given the paramilitaries' depredations, it is crucial for the long-term health of Colombian democracy that the army cut even its indirect ties to them. U.S. aid should also come with human rights considerations and strong monitoring mechanisms attached.

> *"Riches, no matter how ill-gotten, became the goal of many Colombians, and respect for civic rights, education, and honest work declined."*

When President Andrés Pastrana was elected in 1998, he quickly launched peace talks with both FARC and the ELN for the first time in eight years. Following the same script as in 1990, he offered safe havens to the guerrillas to make them feel secure enough to start negotiations. The first block of territory was given to FARC, which received 42,000 square kilometers—the size of Switzerland or Kentucky. But the territory was ceded without many controls, and the move has sparked criticism: this time around, the guerrillas have used their newfound freedom to arrange kidnappings, carry out summary executions, and sponsor coca plantations.

Another block of territory was recently granted to the ELN, and this time, the government tried to correct some of the mistakes it made in dealing with FARC. The ELN's safe haven takes up only 5,000 square kilometers, a bit larger than Long Island, and the zone was offered together with national and international verification mechanisms to prevent any transgressions. Nevertheless, the agreement with the ELN may still produce trouble, since the safe haven lies near areas controlled by the paramilitaries and near important oil pipelines, once the ELN's favorite target.

An Evil Hour

Any discussion of Colombia's current plight has to start with the fact that the war against drugs and the war against the guerrillas run parallel. Outright victory in either is impossible over the near term. So the most sensible course for the government and its foreign partners is a three-track strategy that strives to tamp down the violence of the civil war, limit the role and power of drug interests in Colombia's politics and economics, and lower the demand for drugs abroad.

"The drug class has spread corruption money around Congress and other Colombian institutions and financed the campaign of a former president."

FARC is both a narcotrafficking operation and an insurgent group seeking political power. Its strongholds are also the areas that grow 90 percent of the country's cocaine. Colombians have slowly realized that since drug money can finance a perpetual insurgency, there will be no peace without dealing with the drug plantations. Nor can the current drug-supply networks be dismantled if the guerrillas continue to operate unchallenged and control 120,000 hectares of coca, 12,000 hectares of poppies, and 5,000 hectares of marijuana. Since all groups in the Colombian conflict have independent financing, they can shrug off pressure from outsiders if they wish. Moreover, neither the government nor the rebels have any hope of total victory on the battlefield. For these reasons if no others, the peace process must be nurtured until some mutually acceptable outcome can be reached. Colombians know this, but the country needs the support of the international community as well, which should play the same sort of role in Colombia that it has in such places as the Middle East and Northern Ireland.

Foreigners should be ready to step in to pressure and cajole all sides when the peace process becomes stalemated. Outsiders can assure the rebels, for example, that nothing will happen to them if they lay down their arms. Most members of armed groups fear that once they sign a peace accord and give up their weapons, they will be killed or thrown in jail. These concerns are entirely legitimate, given that during an earlier attempt at peace talks with FARC in the late 1980s, an entire FARC-backed political party was annihilated. More than 3,500 members of that group, the Unión Patriótica, either were murdered or disappeared—a crime that not only increased rebel suspicions but lowered the prospects for the eventual creation of a democratic leftist political party.

Colombia's military also has worries—chiefly that a settlement will be bought with concessions at its expense—that need to be taken into account. Balancing the need to grant amnesties with the need to prosecute war crimes will be difficult, but a start would be the formation of a truth commission like the ones created in South Africa and El Salvador.

The United States could play a more active role in fostering the peace process through the efforts of a special envoy or presidential representative. More American involvement would help bring representatives from the armed groups, the government, and civil society together for serious talks on a negotiated end to the conflict. In the meantime, the international community should use diplomatic pressure and observer missions to help ensure that all sides respect international humanitarian law.

I Want a New Drug Policy

Ideally, at the same time the United States stepped up its diplomacy, it would also change its approach to the other half of the Colombian dilemma, the war on drugs. Current American drug policy emphasizes a unilateral or bilateral approach; what is really needed is a long-term multilateral approach that stresses shared goals, increased cooperation, and sensible compromises.

Between 1989 and 1992, the Colombian government persuaded the United States to meet with Colombia and other drug-producing nations to develop new policies to combat drug trafficking. That effort to forge a multilateral approach died in 1993 when Peruvian President Alberto Fujimori staged an autógolpe, or self-coup, and Colombians elected President Ernesto Samper after a campaign dominated by drug money. The Clinton administration then retreated to the same tired, ineffectual, unilateral certification process—whereby drug-producing nations must demonstrate that they are making major progress in the fight against drugs or face sanctions—that has justly created so much ill will for America in the region. The time has come to revive the multilateral efforts, and include the European Union to boot. Few in Colombia believe that outright legalization would end the problem; just as there is no supply-side panacea, we know that there is no demand-side one, either. Still, Americans' and Europeans' appetite for cocaine helps fuel Colombia's misery, and anything that reduces that appetite helps. The parties on both ends of the equation need to share the blame and work out common goals on how to tackle consumption, production, and distribution.

> *"U.S. aid should . . . come with human rights considerations and strong monitoring mechanisms attached."*

Finally, there is the economy. The Colombian private sector has become less competitive because of the pressures of the insurgency and the drug war. Fair treatment for Colombians would include a trade initiative to let Colombian products enter the U.S. market without tariffs or barriers. This would not be a handout, just a bit of help that will create a demand for Colombia's legal exports as great as that for its drugs. Colombian flowers, shoes, coal, coffee, clothes, and textiles have been slapped with tariffs and trade barriers because they were often used by drug traffickers to smuggle drugs. Today Colombia's industries need fairer treatment. The Central American wars ended with access to the U.S. market for their products. Colombia deserves no less.

None of these policies will bring a swift end to the problems that bedevil Colombia and the region. But together, they might reduce the level of violence, reestablish public order, and lay the groundwork for a negotiated settlement down the road. Without them, even billions of dollars in aid will not be enough.

Assisting Colombia Is in the United States' Best Interest

by Mauricio Vargas

About the author: *Mauricio Vargas is the director of CMI, a national television newscast in Colombia.*

After so many years of enduring a U.S. policy that focused obsessively on drug trafficking to the detriment of the other part of the bilateral agenda, Colombia is beginning to see a timid but welcome change of attitude in political and academic centers in the United States. A much desired and perhaps reachable peace process is beginning to take shape in Colombia, and the accompanying signs coming from the U.S. are encouraging.

To be fair, during the Ernesto Samper administration, 1994-1998, there were signs coming from the north that indicated a disposition to change the tone of the relationship between the two countries. However, the scandal over the disclosure of drug money coming from the Cali drug cartel to finance Samper's presidential campaign severely damaged his credibility. It also narrowed whatever chance he had to succeed on the international scene.

Domestically, the campaign financing drug scandal made it virtually impossible for Samper to engage the different guerrilla groups that operate in the country in a meaningful dialogue for peace. On the international front, whatever attitudinal change the U.S. had envisioned toward Colombia was forsaken during those four years.

The change in focus we now are sensing in U.S. policymakers is not only a positive sign but a very fundamental one. The approach taken over the past years has been a complete failure. The effects of the crop-eradication programs on the coca and poppy fields have been almost nil. The persecution and death of drug lord Pablo Escobar and the imprisonment of the brothers Rodriguez Orejuela brought about a proliferation of smaller cartels whose capos have turned

Reprinted, by permission of the author, from "Bogotá Must First Win the Guerrilla War," by Mauricio Vargas, *Los Angeles Times*, October 23, 1998.

out to be more efficient than the previous ones, albeit less famous.

Perhaps the main reason why the scope of the combat against drug trafficking has been so limited, in spite of the enormous cost it has had on human lives and economic resources in a country as poor as Colombia, is due to the existence of the guerrillas that reign over one-fifth of the national territory.

In many parts of the southern forests, coca and poppy growers not only enjoy the protection of the guerrillas but are actively encouraged by them to increase their trade. The growers are groups of peasants who rely on the guerrillas as their main supporting force. For the guerrillas, the peasants represent the popular base of support they need to dominate the region. Not to mention the fact that the guerrillas make a lot of money protecting the laboratories where the cartels process the drugs.

Using the army and the police to battle the guerrillas on a daily basis distracts the meager resources of the nation and prevents the state from directing the full strength of those two institutions to combating drug trafficking.

Having a guerrilla war in a territory composed of more than 500 out of 1,000 municipalities destabilizes the state and makes the administration of justice in those territories an unmanageable process. The people who live in the region prefer to call the guerrillas to settle their justice issues rather than relying on members of the judiciary system that operates in the rest of the country.

> *"The change in focus we are now sensing in U.S. policymakers is not only a positive sign but a very fundamental one."*

As long as the guerrillas reign in the countryside, it will be impossible for the state to eradicate illicit crops and to destroy the network of cocaine and heroin processing laboratories. As long as there are guerrillas, the focus of the military and the police will remain primarily in the fight against them, and the combat against drug traffickers will remain in the background.

But that's not all. If in spite of the courageous acts of Colombian President Andres Pastrana, who went to the forest to talk to the guerrillas, the peace process fails, then the chances of the war widening increase. That may mean placing in jeopardy the stability of neighboring countries—a real danger.

It is in the best interest of the government and the people of the United States to support the effort to bring peace to Colombia. Only after the laborious disentangling of the guerrilla war can Colombia aspire to win the battle against drug traffickers. Only the pacification of Colombia can guarantee the United States that one of its main allies in the region can free itself of the burden of violence that has so vastly limited its development.

Colombia Deserves Assistance to Combat Drug Trafficking

by Francis Fukuyama

About the author: *Francis Fukuyama is a professor of public policy at George Mason University and author of* The Great Disruption: Human Nature and the Reconstitution of Social Order.

The Clinton administration's proposal to provide $1.57 billion in aid to Colombia to help fight drugs has drawn opposition from many of the same forces that opposed U.S. support to Central America during the Reagan administration. A coterie of human-rights groups have warned of abuses by paramilitary groups said to be working with the Colombian military. Other critics say the aid package will encourage repression, militarize a drug problem better dealt with through treatment and draw the U.S. into a Vietnam-style quagmire.

Support for the package is, by contrast, quite tepid. House Republicans are generally favorable to the administration's proposal; they have even tacked on an additional $500 million. But there is very little genuine enthusiasm for helping Colombia, and a good deal of partisan bickering continues over the proposal's details. Particularly notable is the silence from internationalists on both left and right who fervently supported U.S. involvement in Bosnia and Kosovo.

This indifference is a mistake. Colombia is one of Latin America's oldest continuously functioning democracies, and as such it deserves the same support against the nihilistic forces consuming it as any other democratic American ally during the Cold War, not to speak of nondemocratic proteges like the Kosovars.

Dangerous Misunderstandings

One reason Americans have misunderstood what is at stake in Colombia is that the Clinton administration chooses to portray the struggle as part of the "war on drugs.". . . But while Colombian coca production has increased re-

Reprinted from "Colombia Deserves U.S. Help," by Francis Fukuyama, *The Wall Street Journal*, March 28, 2000, by permission of the author and *The Wall Street Journal*. Copyright © 2000 Dow Jones & Company, Inc. All rights reserved.

cently as producers were driven out of neighboring Peru and Bolivia, the splashy war against the drug cartels in Medellin and Cali has actually subsided.

It has been replaced by a dramatic escalation of one of the Cold War's last remaining insurgencies, waged by two Marxist-Leninist groups, the Revolutionary Armed Forces of Colombia (known by the Spanish acronym FARC) and the National Liberation Army (ELN). These groups have been so isolated in their southern jungle hideouts that they haven't heard of the collapse of socialism. Yet this hasn't stopped them from finding a profitable source of funding in a drug trade that has allowed them to control perhaps 40% of Colombia's territory and to stage spectacular ambushes and kidnappings in the outskirts of Bogota.

Back in Washington, some Democrats object to the U.S. "militarizing" the war by outfitting two new counternarcotics battalions and providing helicopters. In reality, that struggle has been militarized for some time. And nothing—neither development, nor greater democracy, nor a better life for Colombians—can proceed without first solving the security problem.

The stability of democratic institutions in Colombia has potential consequences well beyond its borders. In the last generation, Latin America has been making enormous strides in consolidating democratic institutions and market economies. Economic liberalization started in Chile in the 1980s and continued with the reforms instituted by Carlos Salinas in Mexico, Carlos Menem in Argentina and Fernando Henrique Cardoso in Brazil.

But a new and disturbing pattern has emerged in South America's northern, Andean countries over the last three years. Ecuador saw one president removed from office for mental incompetence and another deposed in a military coup. The country's out-of-control central bank was effectively shut down when the International Monetary Fund concluded it was dealing with a country small enough to allow to fail. Venezuela, meanwhile, elected as president Hugo Chavez, a former army colonel who had launched an unsuccessful military coup against the government of Carlos Andres Perez in 1992.

While Mr. Chavez has acted with punctilious legality this time around, he has also completely rewritten the Venezuelan constitution, denounced the liberalizing reforms initiated by his predecessors and cozied up to the region's old left—including domestic communists, Fidel Castro and the FARC. Thus, should guerillas and drug traffickers in Colombia undermine legitimate institutions there, it will have direct spillover effects in the Andes and

> *"There is very little genuine enthusiasm for helping Colombia, and a good deal of partisan bickering continues over . . . details."*

might signal a broader trend away from democracy throughout Latin America.

It is easy to see why many Americans are leery of involvement in Colombia. There are numerous parallels to Vietnam:

We are being asked to help in a guerilla war fought in a tropical jungle; the government we are supporting, while democratic, has been highly corrupt; and our ally's military is poorly trained and demoralized. The Colombian government has also been supported by unsavory paramilitary units, one of whose leaders appeared on Colombian television recently and explained that his group, like the FARC, receives a substantial portion of its funding from the drug trade. Fear that a U.S. advisory mission will expand into an active combat role leads critics like Ralph Peters to argue against anything more than monetary support.

Yet the likelihood that a mission will expand is greatly overstated. We all remember Vietnam and aren't likely to get similarly bogged down again. A better precedent is U.S. aid for El Salvador in the early 1980s, where Congress explicitly banned advisers from combat. This worked to the benefit of all: The U.S. military was forced to think creatively about counterinsurgency training rather than following its predilections for overwhelming force, while the Salvadoran government got the clear message that the war was its to lose.

The biggest questions today are whether the Colombian military, underfunded and lacking in prestige, can be turned around with better training and equipment, and whether it can distance itself adequately from the paramilitaries. We won't know unless we try; we can always back out.

Colombian democracy is far from perfect, but it is a lot better than any of the alternatives. President Andres Pastrana's predecessor, Ernesto Samper, was highly corrupt, having accepted money from cartels. But Mr. Pastrana, elected in 1998, came to office with a clean record and a reformist mandate. If anything, he has proved too well-intentioned, engaging the FARC in what amounts to joint therapy sessions with Wall Streeters and European parliamentarians. He has offered them plenty of carrots, but he still lacks a stick. Still, it is not crazy to think that, suitably bolstered by a military option, a political solution may some day be possible.

Americans must remember that we are responsible for many of Colombia's horrific problems since we are the ones consuming all that cocaine. If we are not willing to legalize drugs, we should not kid ourselves that we can simply wash our hands of the problems of this troubled fellow democracy.

More Assistance Is Needed to Combat Drug Trafficking in Colombia

by Gordon Barthos

About the author: *Gordon Barthos writes foreign affairs editorials for the* Toronto Star, *a Canadian newspaper.*

Life is cheap in cocaine—and heroin—rich Colombia.

Three farmers were murdered in January 2001—for their sneakers.

It wasn't theft. It was politics.

The men were sporting runners from a shipment hijacked by Marxist guerrillas. They ran into some right-wing paramilitary killers.

The killers didn't much care whether the farmers were guerrilla fighters, sympathizers or customers.

Colombia's political war has taken 35,000 lives in the past decade, and displaced 2 million. But it's also inherently one of the most violent societies anywhere, with 35,000 non-political murders a year.

Strapping its military boots on, the United States has just waded into this mess.

Plan Colombia

Washington is spending $1.3 billion to train 2,300 Colombian troops, to equip them with Blackhawk and other combat helicopters and to improve their tactical intelligence-gathering.

President Andres Pastrana, a reform-minded democrat, sent the troops into Putumayo province, a guerrilla stronghold where half the coca crop is produced, to back up the police who are spraying herbicides like glyphosate (Roundup) on coca and poppy fields, and dismantling drug labs.

It's the aggressive phase of Pastrana's $7.5 billion Plan Colombia effort to bust up an unholy alliance of guerrillas and narco-traffickers, to cut drug production in half by 2005, and to restore a semblance of order to the country,

Reprinted, with the permission of the Toronto Star Syndicate, from "Shrugging Off Colombia's Anguish," by Gordon Barthos, *The Toronto Star*, January 12, 2001.

which produces most of the world's cocaine and much of its heroin.

Colombia's economy runs to about $100 billion a year. Some $20 billion may flow from drugs. Critics of the U.S. military aid decry it as a massive, covert drive to help Pastrana beat back Marxists under the pretext of waging a war on drugs.

But those critics, who range from Roman Catholic clerics to Amnesty International to peace groups and other reputable voices, may be giving U.S. policymakers credit for bigger designs than they have.

It's hard to imagine that a few Blackhawk helicopters will defeat the guerrillas. They've been waging war for 40 years or more, financed by drugs, kidnapping and extortion. Nor will the choppers frighten the narco-barons out of business.

Moreover, some of the U.S. money at least is earmarked as well for rural development and to encourage farmers to plant other crops.

If anything Plan Colombia aims low.

Busting the Nexus

Pastrana would be happy simply to arrest Colombia's fast-deteriorating security situation by making things hot enough so that the narco-barons who operate on guerrilla turf have an incentive to take their drug labs and money to other, quieter areas, thus squeezing the guerrilla cash flow.

One senior U.S. official calls it "busting the nexus."

Otherwise a full-blown, heavily armed narco-state the size of Switzerland may emerge in the northwestern corner of South America, on the 40 per cent of Colombia that the guerrillas control.

"What this assistance from the U.S. government does is give President Pastrana an additional card to play as he works the peace process with the Colombian guerrillas," Bill Brownfield stated in January 2001. He's deputy assistant secretary of state for Western hemisphere affairs in the U.S. State Department.

"It gives him the opportunity to say to them that you may subject yourselves to this additional military and law enforcement pressure, or you may break your links with the narcotic traffickers and engage in serious peace negotiations."

The George W. Bush administration is considering pumping another $1 billion or so into fighting drugs in the region in 2001, with half going to Colombia and half to neighbouring Andean states where the drug lords may try to set up shop.

Critics of Plan Colombia fault the U.S. for fighting its war on the backs

> *"Colombia's political war has taken 35,000 lives in the past decade, and displaced 2 million."*

of peasants, instead of attacking an insatiable American demand for these drugs.

The Colombian police have doused not only drug crops with herbicides, but also adjacent farms. Even villagers. People are fleeing.

Meanwhile, villagers and farmers are getting squeezed by the rebels, by coke dealers and by right-wing paramilitary forces, all of whom demand loyalty and support at gunpoint.

Critics decry this "militarization" of the landscape. They'd prefer to see more effort put into Pastrana's faltering attempts to coax the guerrillas into peace talks, into making sure the military and its murderous and increasingly autonomous paramilitary allies respect human rights, and into rural development and crop swaps.

Pastrana always hoped to do this.

Failed Promises

But Colombia's fickle friends have been slow to deliver promised help.

The Europeans, for instance, talked about pledging $1 billion for peace, justice and development, but have provided just $250 million, and that over six years.

Canada, while praising Pastrana, coughs up a paltry $13 million a year in aid.

Whatever Ottawa makes of American military policy in Colombia, they could be doing more, instead of wringing their hands in dismay.

That's what Beatriz Jaramillo de Gonzalez urged. She's a human rights worker from Medellin, a drug cartel centre.

"People are dying, and no one cares," she said.

She asked Ottawa to give Pastrana political encouragement. To forgive Colombia's debt. To provide generous aid.

And to express indignation at the barbarities committed against ordinary people for ideology, and profit.

Until countries like Canada are prepared to invest more in Colombia's struggling farmers, Marxist guerrillas will have easy recruits and drug lords will have willing helpers.

And one of Latin America's oldest democracies will slowly collapse.

Increased Aid to Colombia's Military Will Not Reduce Drug Trafficking

by Winifred Tate

About the author: *Winifred Tate is senior fellow at the Washington Office on Latin America (WOLA), where she analyzes Colombian and U.S. counternarcotics policy.*

The long-neglected conflict in Colombia is emerging as Latin America's major crisis and pulling the United States ever more deeply into an unwinnable war. Escalating political violence, an entrenched insurgency, increasing illicit drug production and growing concern from Colombia's neighbors about the conflict spilling over have policymakers in Washington searching for a solution to the problems besetting Colombia.

Many U.S. policymakers and military leaders are calling for increased U.S. aid for the Colombian military. But this will only serve to pull the United States closer to the most abusive military forces in the hemisphere without reducing illicit drug production or contributing to stability and democracy in that beleaguered country.

Though the Colombian army has declared itself "reformed," the nation's military is far from a new institution. Military collusion with paramilitary activity on a local and regional level continues, and paramilitary violence has escalated. These groups target alleged guerrilla sympathizers, but their net of terror has been cast wide over a growing number of Colombian peace leaders and members of civil society. More than 400 people were killed or "disappeared" in the first three months of 1999 alone, and tens of thousands more have been forced to flee their homes.

Reprinted, by permission of the author, from "Increased U.S. Military Aid to Colombia Won't Curb Drug Trafficking," by Winifred Tate, *San Francisco Chronicle*, August 19, 1999, p. A-25.

Chapter 3

Colombia's Corrupt Military

Two generals have been cashiered because of evidence of participating in human rights abuses, but the army continues to harbor many officers linked to rights violations, including high-level commanders. General Rafael Hernandez Lopez, for example, was named chief of staff of the Colombian Armed Forces, despite a pending investigation for his alleged participation in the 1996 kidnapping and murder of a guerrilla leader's family member. Human rights organizations and Colombian judicial authorities have gathered extensive evidence of his implication in numerous human rights violations, including summary executions, forced disappearances, rape and torture committed by soldiers under his command. Increased military aid is not likely to improve the military's human rights performance.

In 1990, the United States sent a team of military advisers to Colombia to review that country's military intelligence organizations and recommend changes. Colombia's military intelligence apparatus was reorganized, and clandestine intelligence networks were established that, in at least one case, functioned as paramilitary death squads. One such group, Naval Intelligence Network No. 7, was responsible for the murder of more than 50 civilians. Five military officials, including Lt. Col. Rodrigo Quinonez, were found guilty of creating and financing this paramilitary group in order to murder local opposition leaders and union organizers. Quinonez remains on active duty, with only a letter of reprimand in his file.

"More than 400 people were killed or 'disappeared' in the first three months of 1999 alone."

In 1999, drug czar Barry McCaffrey requested $40 million in aid for "regional intelligence programs," part of a nearly $600 million emergency aid package for Colombia. This despite concerns substantiated by a General Accounting Office report revealing that U.S. intelligence shared with the Colombian military lacks mechanisms "to ensure that it is not being used for other than counternarcotics purposes."

Focus on Human Rights

Support for the Colombian military is pulling the United States into the quagmire of a protracted and dirty counterinsurgency struggle, with no clear policy objective. There is no evidence that focusing counternarcotics efforts on battling the country's largest guerrilla group, the Revolutionary Armed Forces of Colombia or FARC, will reduce coca production. In fact, right-wing paramilitary groups, linked to the Colombian security forces, are more deeply involved in drug trafficking. Aerial fumigation has pushed a desperate peasant population further into the jungle—or into the arms of the insurgency.

While only Colombians can resolve their crisis, the international community—and particularly the United States—can and should do much to support an eventual negotiated settlement. We should begin by correcting the overwhelming imbalance in U.S. aid: more than $230 million in predominantly military assistance for counternarcotics operations, less than $10 million for development, judicial and law enforcement and human rights.

On March 10, 1999, President Clinton apologized for the U.S. role in Guatemala's long internal conflict, saying that "support for military forces or intelligence units which engaged in violent and widespread repression . . . was wrong, and the United States must not repeat that mistake." Now, . . . we risk repeating that mistake by intervening in a counterinsurgency war that the United States cannot win.

Clear support for human rights and civilian democracy will prevent the need for future apologies to Colombians who have suffered enough in the name of misguided counternarcotics policies.

The United States Should Not Assist Colombia's War Against Drug Traffickers

by Alexander Cockburn

About the author: *Alexander Cockburn authors a column called "Beat the Devil" for the* Nation, *a biweekly journal of opinion.*

Anyone wanting a vivid snapshot of the rubble of US policy toward Latin America should glance at Colombia, where the Clinton Administration now has one foot over the brink of a military intervention strongly reminiscent of John Kennedy's initial deployments in Vietnam.

Colombia is in economic free fall, and, as Larry Birns of the Council on Hemispheric Affairs remarks, the only comfort its beleaguered inhabitants can seize upon is that the velocity of this collapse is at least slower than that of neighboring Ecuador, now experiencing its worst economic slump in seventy years. Colombia is currently suffering negative growth, has an official unemployment rate of 19 percent and an actual unemployment rate probably more than twice that figure. Austerity programs imposed by the IMF and World Bank have closed off any hope for that half of the country's population that lives below the poverty line.

It shouldn't be this way. With a diversity of exports, Colombia could have one of the strongest economies of Latin America. But it's the same old story. Down the years every US Administration has sent arms and advisers to prop up Colombia's elites. US-assisted repression in Colombia has been spectacularly appalling. According to the Permanent Committee for the Defense of Human Rights in Colombia, 3,832 political murders were perpetrated in 1998, the bulk of them done by the army, police and right-wing paramilitaries. To lend a sense of perspective, this is about twice the death toll in Kosovo that prompted charges of Serbian genocide and that helped whip up sentiment for NATO's war on Serbia.

Reprinted from "Colombia: Our Next Guatemala?" by Alexander Cockburn, *The Nation*, August 23, 1999, by permission of the author.

Increased Aid

The US government prepared to escalate vastly the money and weapons going to the Colombian military in 2000, far beyond the $289 million in already-scheduled assistance in 1999, making Colombia the third-largest recipient of American aid, after Israel and Egypt. Congress has already appropriated another half-billion for the drug war, with much of it going to Colombia. General Barry McCaffrey, former director of the White House Office of National Drug Control Policy, asked for a further $1 billion for the drug war over the next three years, said sum to go to the Andean countries, with about half to Colombia alone. The Colombian military requested yet another $500 million.

McCaffrey's request puts an end to any pretense that there is somehow a distinction between US backing of counterinsurgency and of counterdrug activities. A Congressional amendment has forbidden US military aid to go to Latin American army units with a documented record of human rights abuses. But in the pellmell rush to throw money at Colombia's military, such niceties are being cast over the side.

Rebel Groups

The immediate cause of panic is the strength of Colombia's main insurgency, run by the Revolutionary Armed Forces of Colombia (FARC). In a peace-feeler in 1999, President Andres Pastrana effectively ceded the FARC control over a 16,000-square-mile slab of south-central Colombia, about the size of Switzerland. The Clinton Administration was not entirely unsympathetic to this overture, at least until a FARC commander made the brutal and summary decision to execute the three indigenous rights activists—Ingrid Washinawatok, Lahe'ena'e Gay and Terence Freitas—who were working in the eastern Arauca state on behalf of the U'wa Indians. The FARC did admit responsibility but thereafter refused any of Washington's requests, such as turning over the relevant commander. The FARC says it has to be vigilant against spies and will regard US personnel as legitimate targets.

Pastrana's decision to cede de facto control of a slice of territory to FARC infuriated the military, which has been increasingly humiliated by guerrilla strength that, in 1999, brought FARC forces as close as twenty-five miles from Bogotá. With a nominal force of 40,000, the Colombian Army currently has around 6,000 to 7,000

> *"Colombia is in economic freefall."*

frontline troops who are paid only a third of what FARC's fighters receive. FARC can afford such a military budget because of its taxes on drug cultivation and shipments in the zones it controls.

For their part the FARC's leaders have questioned whether Pastrana has the ability to deliver on any negotiated settlement. Not without reason. Every single guerrilla group agreeing to lay down its arms and enter the conventional political arena has seen its members slaughtered by the paramilitaries controlled by the army and the police.

Support in Washington

There is a powerful lobby in Washington for pouring money into counterinsurgency in Colombia. McCaffrey spouts pieties about separating the drug war from counterinsurgency, but says simultaneously that the United States is duty bound to assist the Colombian government to beat off any threat. Colombian police chief José Serrano has forged close links with Senator Jesse Helms and Representative Ben Gilman, who head the foreign relations committees considering the requests for big new appropriations to the Colombian military. The Pentagon is sending planes and personnel into Colombia. The US Army's intelligence-gathering de Havilland RC-7 that crashed into a Colombian mountain in the early hours of July 23, 1999, was almost certainly monitoring FARC deployments, with such information being relayed to the Colombian military.

There are two faces to US policy toward Latin America, both repulsive. The first is that of economic neoliberalism, preaching the virtues of uninhibited trade, open markets, privatization, structural adjustment. On the ground, across Latin America, we see the consequence: social devastation in thirty-one kleptocracies, all corrupt, many bankrupt. The alternate face, whose baleful glare is now fixed upon Colombia, is that of military re-

> *"Every single guerrilla group agreeing to lay down its arms . . . has seen its members slaughtered by the paramilitaries."*

pression. Bolstered with fresh US cash, the Colombian military is probably planning a direct coup unless Pastrana takes a hard-line stance against FARC and other guerrilla insurgencies. For thirty years the United States underwrote genocide in Guatemala. With 30,000 civilians already killed, Colombia could become its successor. Congress should veto any aid or comfort.

The United States Should Not Support Colombia's Brutal Military

by *The Progressive*

About the author: The Progressive *is a weekly journal primarily concerned with civil rights and liberties, peace, and social justice.*

Torn by civil war, Colombia is quickly becoming another chapter in the ignominious tome of U.S. meddling in Latin America. Today, U.S. policy toward Colombia is almost exactly at the same spot where U.S. policy toward El Salvador was in 1980: U.S. military aid to a brutal government is increasing dramatically; U.S. "advisers" are on the ground, "professionalizing" the armed forces; U.S. officials are sharing "intelligence" with a military that has one of the worst human rights records in the hemisphere.

"More than 1,000 civilians were killed [in 1998] by the security forces or paramilitary groups operating with their support or acquiescence," Amnesty International says in its 1999 annual report. "Many were tortured before being killed. At least 150 people 'disappeared.' Human rights activists were threatened and attacked; at least six were killed. 'Death squad'-style killings continued in urban areas. Several army officers were charged in connection with human rights violations; many others continued to evade accountability."

The State Department itself acknowledged in February 1999 that Colombian "government forces continued to commit numerous, serious abuses, including extrajudicial killings." Yet the United States is boosting its military aid to just these forces.

"You are unwittingly complicitous in some of the worst mass murders in the hemisphere today," says Carlos Salinas, Amnesty International's advocacy director for Latin America and the Caribbean. "If you liked El Salvador, you're going to love Colombia. It's the same death squads, the same military aid, and the same whitewash from Washington."

Reprinted, with permission, from "Stop the War on Colombia," an editorial in the September 1999 issue of *The Progressive*.

Chapter 3

The War on Drugs Excuse

The only difference between El Salvador in 1980 and Colombia in 1999 is the pretext. Since the Cold War is over and fighting communism is passé, Washington needed a new excuse for helping a brutal Latin American security apparatus. That excuse is the war on drugs.

Technically, all of the military aid that the United States is sending to Colombia goes for counternarcotics efforts. And the amount of that aid is huge. Colombia is the leading recipient of U.S. military aid in Latin America, and the third largest in the world, behind only Israel and Egypt. Between 1990 and 1998, Colombia's police and military received $625 million in counternarcotics aid. In 1999, Colombia received $289 million from Washington.

And now, the Administration—egged on by Republicans and by drug czar Barry McCaffrey (who, by the way, used to head up the U.S. Southern Command, the Latin American outpost of the Pentagon)—is considering an additional $1 billion in emergency aid primarily for Colombia.

But the Colombian police and military are not fighting a drug war. They are fighting an old-fashioned civil war against leftwing rebels who are gaining strength. This is the emergency the Pentagon worries about—not drugs. Colombia is strategically located, bordering both the Caribbean Sea and the Pacific Ocean. And it has vast oil and mineral reserves that multinational corporations have been exploiting for years, often under the armed guard of the Colombian military. These are the interests at play here.

"Military aid is being given in the name of drugs but in reality it is to keep control of the territory of Colombia," says Cecilia Zarate-Laun, the co-founder and program director of the Colombia Support Network, based in Madison, Wisconsin.

That drugs are not the issue is easily provable. It's not just the rebels who are involved in the drug trade. The Colombian military and its allied paramilitaries are also deeply implicated.

Corruption in the Ranks

In November 1999, for instance, to the embarrassment of the Clinton Administration, a Colombian air force plane landed in Fort Lauderdale with six Colombian military officers on board. But they weren't the only passengers. According to *The Washington Post*, the plane "was carrying 1,639 pounds of cocaine inside pallets in the aircraft's spacious cargo hold. . . . The cocaine had a wholesale value of $12.7 million." Heroin was also found.

Even a U.S. General Accounting Office (GAO) report, dated June 1999, notes that "drug-related corruption existed in all branches of the government," including the military.

Interestingly, that report, entitled "Narcotics Threat from Colombia Continues to Grow," places the blame for most of the drug trafficking on two parties: the rebels and the paramilitaries. "Insurgent and paramilitary organizations are increasingly becoming involved in drug-trafficking-related activities and are controlling more territory," it said. Some paramilitary leaders "have become major drug traffickers."

Yet the United States is financing a so-called drug war only against the rebels, and not against the paramilitaries. "In theory, we would assume that there would be an armed confrontation with both," says Amnesty's Salinas. "Yet there has not been one clash, one armed confrontation between the army and these paramilitary forces."

Instead, the Colombian government shields the paramilitaries. "We often find that when the paramilitary groups are attacked by the opposition, the army just happens to show up," says Salinas. "They don't show up to combat the paramilitaries; they show up to combat the armed opposition groups. The paramilitaries are doing joint operations with the military. On repeated occasions, truckloads of paramilitaries have committed massacres in places where there is a large police and military presence. These massacres go on for three or more hours, with heavy gunfire, without any attempt by the police or the military to stop the carnage. How does something like that happen? It just doesn't happen unless there's collusion."

Some of that collusion comes courtesy of the U.S. government, as Frank Smyth reported for *The Progressive* in June 1998 in an article entitled "Still Seeing Red." In Colombia in 1991, "the CIA financed new military intelligence networks," which "incorporated illegal paramilitary groups into their ranks and fostered death squads," Smyth wrote. While part of the CIA was fighting drugs, other units were helping paramilitary drug dealers. "The CIA bears some responsibility for the proliferation of drug trafficking in the Magdalena Valley since it supported rightist counterinsurgency forces who run drugs," said Smyth.

> *"Military aid is being given in the name of drugs but in reality it is to keep control of the territory of Colombia."*

Drug War or Civil War

Now, as the U.S. government is increasingly becoming involved in Colombia's civil war, it is beginning to tip its hand. It is having difficulty keeping up the pretense of helping Colombia fight drugs, as it blatantly helps the military wage war against the guerrillas.

"U.S. embassy officials have decided to routinely provide intelligence information related to the insurgents to Colombian units under control of the Joint Task Force [a unit of the Colombian police and military]," the GAO report noted, adding: "They do not have a system to ensure that it is not being used for other than counternarcotics purposes."

For the results of this intelligence sharing, check out the *New York Times* of July 17, 1999. General Charles Wilhelm, head of the Southern Command, "acknowledged that American and Colombian military officials had been in constant communication throughout the weekend, appearing to confirm Colombian news reports that devastating bombing attacks on the guerrillas were based on information provided by the United States."

Such aid could not be coming at a worse time. Colombia's president, Andrés Pastrana, has gone out on a

> *"The Colombian government shields the paramilitaries."*

limb to open negotiations with the rebels and even to cede territory to them on a de facto basis. U.S. military aid undermines his position and strengthens the Colombian armed forces, which have no interest in peace.

"For the first time, there is the possibility of peace between the guerrillas and the government," José Antonio Lopez, the former mayor of Apartadó, a city in the northwest corner of Colombia, told *The Progressive* on a visit in May 1999. Lopez is one of the few surviving members of the Patriotic Union, an opposition political party that was wiped out by the paramilitaries in the late 1980s and early 1990s. Some 5,000 members were assassinated. ("I look back and I don't see anyone," he says. "Almost all of them are dead. When I see pictures of the rallies we had in the 1980s, they are a roster of people who were killed.")

Lopez warned that "the biggest enemy Pastrana has is the military, and if the peace process doesn't show results quickly, the space will evaporate."

Preferring War to Peace

So what is the U.S. view of the peace process? Pretty dim, according to the GAO report. "U.S. officials have expressed concerns about the peace process and its potential impact on counternarcotics operations," it states. Then comes an all-purpose criticism: "The government lacks a clearly defined negotiating strategy." And finally, the report says the Administration is worried that peace may actually break out: "U.S. officials are concerned that U.S. and Colombian counternarcotics efforts could be limited by an indefinite extension of the ninety-day cease-fire zone or by expanding the area of the demilitarized zone."

When the U.S. government goes on record opposing cease-fire zones and demilitarized zones, it becomes clear that Washington prefers war to peace.

This is not to say that the Colombian rebels are angels. They're not. And we should not romanticize them. They involve themselves in the drug trade. Worse, they commit atrocities of their own. The Revolutionary Armed Forces of Colombia (FARC) killed three Americans in early March 1999 who were helping an indigenous group organize schools. And the FARC has killed many Colombian civilians, as well.

"They kill civilians randomly, and they kidnap people and ruin families," says Zarate-Laun of the Colombia Support Network.

"Certainly, the guerrillas have committed many abuses of international law," Father Javier Giraldo, author of *Colombia: The Genocidal Democracy*, told *The*

Progressive on a visit in April. Father Giraldo, who was the founder and executive director of the Intercongregational Commission for Justice and Peace in Colombia, is now in exile because of rightwing death threats. "Sometimes the guerrillas commit human rights violations almost as atrocious as the paramilitaries." Giraldo's book demonstrates that the lion's share of the tens of thousands of political killings in Colombia from 1988 to 1995 were committed by the paramilitaries.

Given the mess that is Colombia's thirty-year war, what is to be done?

"The international community must become involved in the peace process and pressure the U.S. government to immediately stop military aid to Colombia," Zarate-Laun says. "Giving military aid to Colombia is like pouring gasoline on a fire."

Zarate-Laun also says that Colombia's ruling sector must be willing to budge. "If the upper classes don't change their attitudes, the problems will never be solved," she says. "They want to destroy the guerrillas, but they have no understanding of why there are guerrillas in the first place."

For her outspokenness, Zarate-Laun received a snide letter this spring from Colonel J.C. Hiett, then head of U.S. military operations in Colombia. "I just wish you knew what you were talking about! . . . Last time I looked, there are five countries that are neighbors of Colombia—and they are already having problems with the spillover effects of the guerrilla problem in Colombia," Hiett wrote. "Oh, by the way, 40 percent of the money the U.S. makes in international trade is with Latin America, and we get more oil from Venezuela (Colombia border country) than we do from the Mideast now. Better think about the U.S. economic interests in the future before you propose we let the guerrillas take over."

Hiett, incidentally, stepped aside in early August after his wife, Laurie Anne Hiett, was named in a criminal complaint in Brooklyn with conspiracy to distribute cocaine in the United States. Her lawyer denies the charge. This spring, according to the *New York Times* of August 7, Laurie Anne Hiett allegedly sent six packages of cocaine by diplomatic mail from the U.S. embassy in Bogotá to New York. Hiett says she didn't know what was in the packages and had mailed them "at the behest of her husband's chauffeur," the *Times* said.

> *"When the U.S. government goes on record opposing cease-fire zones and demilitarized zones, it becomes clear that Washington prefers war to peace."*

On the urgent issue of U.S. military aid to Colombia, the Democrats have been largely silent. [Then] President Clinton bowed to pressure from the Pentagon, McCaffrey, and Republicans. And liberals in Congress are almost nowhere to be seen.

"The Democrats have been very, very passive on this," says Zarate-Laun. She says that Representative Sam Farr, Democrat of California, and Representative Tammy Baldwin, Democrat of Wisconsin, have been the only two Democrats who have spoken up against U.S. policy there. "The rest are blind."

Farr, who was in the Peace Corps in Colombia from 1964 to 1966, says, "We've never given a clear message to the Colombians as to what we want. The first thing we should tell them is, 'You've got to negotiate a peace, whatever that takes.'" Farr is ambivalent about aid to the Colombian military. "More money to the military will not be the answer," he says. But he is not opposed to some money for "modernizing" the military, so long as it is conditioned on respect for human rights.

Baldwin, who visited Colombia in 1993 as part of a sister-city exchange between Apartadó and Madison, Wisconsin, was surprised to find "how lopsided the perception is" in Congress about Colombia. "There is a very limited focus on some trade issues and the war on drugs. There is not much inquiry into the side effects of our current policies or the chaos, politically and militarily, that our policies exacerbate."

Abandon Military Assistance

She believes the United States should "abandon military aid" to Colombia. "It is so clear to me that U.S. military aid and equipment are being used for things far removed from the war on drugs," she says. "My concern is that increased military aid will take the peace process off track, and increased military training and equipment will be used by the paramilitaries to terrorize citizens who might promote peace, human rights, and real democracy."

When the Reagan Administration supported the Salvadoran military and the Contras in Nicaragua, concerned citizens in this country rallied in opposition. Effective grassroots organizing sprang up in churches, on campuses, among the unions, and in municipalities around the nation. A similar mobilization is needed today if we are to prevent further carnage in Colombia.

Our government has no right to be supporting the brutal military there. U.S. aid should be cut off immediately. And instead of pooh-poohing the peace process that Pastrana has courageously undertaken, the U.S. government should unequivocally support it.

But that is not in the interests of those who make U.S. policy. They still believe in annihilating rebels, not negotiating with them. They still demand compliant governments in Latin America that will do the bidding of U.S. companies. And they still rely on Latin American militaries, no matter how gruesome their records, as the natural allies of Washington.

These have been the constants of U.S. policy in Latin America for this entire century. The only variable today is the rhetorical one about fighting the drug war. It, however, is but the flimsiest of rationales.

Chapter 4

How Can Drug Trafficking Be Combated?

CURRENT CONTROVERSIES

Chapter Preface

The international drug trade thrives on the overwhelmingly lucrative nature of the black market. Drug enforcement officials estimate that the international drug trade generates $300 to $400 billion annually. The United States contributes approximately 80 percent of drug traffickers' income, despite enforcing one of the strictest antidrug policies in the world. Regardless of increases in antidrug funding and staffing, drug use in the United States has steadily increased since 1992, and officials claim that the drug supply increases by about 350 pounds every day. Much debate surrounding the effectiveness of the current war on drugs has led to controversial proposals on how drugs and drug trafficking can be combated.

Many argue that the war on drugs mirrors the alcohol prohibition era at the beginning of the twentieth century and has been just as unsuccessful. According to David D. Boaz, vice president of the Cato Institute, "One of the broader lessons [government] should have learned is that prohibition laws ought to be judged according to real-world effects, not their promised benefits. If Congress will subject the Federal drug laws to that standard, it will recognize that the drug war is not the answer to problems associated with drug use." Boaz and others maintain that drug prohibition causes more harm to society than drugs because of the lucrative income and subsequent violent crime it engenders. Illegal drugs encourage gang-related crime by fostering disputes over drug trafficking territory, which also threaten the lives of law enforcement officers summoned to maintain peace.

Others maintain that ending drug prohibition would encourage people to use drugs. Many claim that because drug use encourages violence, the increased number of drug users would lead to more crime. According to editor Theodore Dalrymple, "If it is true that the consumption of these drugs in itself predisposes to criminal behavior . . . , it is also possible that the effect on the rate of criminality of this rise in consumption would swamp the decrease that resulted from decriminalization. We would have just as much crime in aggregate as before, but many more addicts." Dalrymple and others argue that prohibition is the most effective way to protect society from the harmful effects of drugs.

Whether drugs should be legalized is one of the issues discussed in the following chapter on how drug trafficking can be combated.

Hemispheric Efforts Can Combat Drug Trafficking

by Barry McCaffrey

About the author: *Barry McCaffrey is a retired four-star general and served as the director of the Office of National Drug Control Policy (ONDCP) from 1996 to 2001.*

Although no single issue dominates our hemispheric agenda, the overall problem of illegal drugs and related crimes represents a direct threat to the health and well-being of the peoples of the [Western] hemisphere. All of us recognize that we cannot afford to let the demand for, and cultivation, production, distribution, trafficking, and sale of illicit narcotics and psycho-tropic substances interfere with the aspirations of our peoples. Illegal drugs inflict staggering costs on our societies. They kill and sicken our people, sap productivity, drain economies, threaten the environment, and undermine democratic institutions and international order. Drugs are a direct attack on our children and grandchildren. If we are to make inroads against this growing problem, we shall only do so collectively. We can make progress by formulating a common understanding of the problems posed by drug production, trafficking, and consumption and by developing cooperative approaches and solutions. . . .

The consequences of illegal drug use have been devastating within the United States. We estimate that in this decade alone, drug use has cost our society more than 100,000 dead and some $300 billion. Each year, more than 500,000 Americans go to hospital emergency rooms because of drug-induced problems. Our children view drugs as the most important problem they face. Drugs and crime threaten all Americans, not just city residents, the poor, or minorities. Americans from every social and economic background, race, and ethnic group are concerned about the interrelated problems of crime, violence, and drugs. We fear the violence that surrounds drug markets. We abhor the effect it has on our children's lives. Americans are especially concerned about the increased use of drugs by young people. Today, dangerous drugs like cocaine, heroin, and methamphetamines are cheaper and more potent than they were at the height of

Excerpted from "Hemispheric Drug Control: Fighting Drug Production and Trafficking," Barry McCaffrey's speech to the Twenty-first Regular Session of the Inter-American Drug Abuse Control Commission, Organization of American States, Washington, DC, April 9, 1997.

our domestic drug problem fifteen or twenty years ago. In Arizona, ninety percent of homicides in 1996 were related to methamphetamines. No nation can afford such devastating social, health, and criminal consequences.

Demand: The Root Cause of the Drug Problem

No one should doubt that the demand for illegal drugs lies at the heart of the global drug problem. We in the United States are cognizant that we are a big part of the demand side of the drug equation. However, the percentage of our citizens that consumes drugs is not the central problem. Currently, about six percent of our population, or twelve million Americans, use drugs—a fifty percent reduction from 1979's twenty-five million. Even the number of casual cocaine users is down seventy-five percent over the past decade. There are probably 600,000 heroin addicts in the United States. They represent but a fraction of the world's opium/heroin addicts and consume less than two percent of the global heroin production capacity. A total of about 3.6 million Americans, or less than two percent of our population, is addicted to illegal drugs. This drug usage causes fourteen thousand deaths and costs $67 billion each year.

The problem is that American drug users have enormous quantities of disposable income. A crack addict in New York can afford a $350 a week habit or steal with relative ease $3,000 or more worth of property to maintain that habit. Indeed, Americans spend about $50 billion a year on illegal drugs. Of the estimated three hundred metric tons of cocaine smuggled into the United States every year, the wholesale value at U.S. points of entry is $10 billion. The retail value of that cocaine on our streets is $30 billion. These enormous sums are the reason criminal organizations dominate international traffic in illegal drugs, threaten our communities, and attack our institutions. All of us should recognize that the traffickers of cocaine, heroin, and the other drugs of abuse are actively seeking to develop new markets. If any country successfully reduces consumption of drugs that remain available, these drugs will find new markets. The new markets, along with the addicts and devastation that accompany them, will increasingly be found in those countries that produce the drugs and those through which they transit.

The U.S. National Drug Control Policy recognizes this reality and prioritizes our efforts accordingly. Our number one goal is to prevent the sixty-eight million Americans under eighteen years of age from becoming a new generation of addicts. We find it unacceptable that drug use rates doubled among our youth from 1992 to 1997; we must and will reverse this trend. While we know that we can't arrest our way out of the drug problem, we will continue to uphold our severe drug laws. A million and-a-half Americans are now behind bars, many for drug law violations.

> *"Drugs are a direct attack on our children and grandchildren."*

More than a million additional Americans are arrested for drug offenses every year. Incarceration is entirely appropriate for many drug-related crimes. There must be strong incentives to stay clear of drug trafficking, and prison sentences can motivate people to obey the law. Our challenge is to address the problem of chronic drug use by bringing drug testing, assessment, referral, treatment, and supervision within the oversight of the U.S. criminal justice system. We are doing so by increasing the number of drug courts that oversee treatment and rehabilitation for drug law violators and by validating ONDCP's "Break the Cycle" concept. As a nation, we are optimistic that we can substantially reduce the demand for illegal drugs in the United States. . . .

Drugs Are a Shared Problem

We recognize that domestic efforts by themselves cannot address what is fundamentally a global problem fueled by powerful, international criminal organizations. All our countries are affected by the drug problem, but not necessarily in the same ways. For some, the most pressing issue is drug consumption. For others, it may be drug-related violence and corruption. Some countries are affected by illicit production or trafficking. Other countries are beset by all these problems. No country is immune. . . .

By any measure, the United States and Mexico have made significant progress in our joint efforts to face up to the drug problem. Whether we speak of investigations of drug trafficking organizations, anti-smuggling projects, crop-eradication efforts, demand-reduction programs, or anti-crime legislation, our record of cooperation is substantial.

> *"Domestic efforts by themselves cannot address what is fundamentally a global problem fueled by powerful, international criminal organizations."*

Former president Ernesto Zedillo made an obvious commitment to political, legal, and institutional reform and was dedicated to fighting drug trafficking—which he identified as the principal threat to Mexico's national security. Under his leadership, Mexican drug seizures increased notably, with marijuana seizures up forty percent over 1994 and opium-related seizures up forty-one percent. Cocaine, methamphetamine, and precursor chemical seizures also rose significantly.

No other nation has eradicated as many hectares of illegal drugs as has Mexico. Our extensive counterdrug cooperation occurs under the rubric of the U.S./Mexico High Level Contact Group for Drug Control. This bilateral drug control policy group was established in March 1996 and has enabled us to advance our collective effort to thwart drug trafficking and the demand for drugs in both nations.

Our two great nations share many drug problems. However, we have resolved to address them forthrightly while affirming our commitment to the principles of international law, particularly those of national sovereignty, territorial integrity, and non-intervention in the internal affairs of other countries. . . .

As suggested by [then] President Bill Clinton's March 1997 report to Congress on the status of International Drug Trafficking and Abuse, international cooperation requires further strengthening. Illicit poppy cultivation for opium increased eleven percent globally from 1994 to 1995, doubling in one country from 1992 [to 1997]. Ominously for the United States, our Drug Enforcement Agency estimates that Colombia was the source of sixty percent of the heroin seized in

> *"The world community cannot allow international criminal organizations to gain a foothold in any country."*

the United States in 1996. Ten years ago, there was no opium growing in Colombia. Many valiant Colombians have since died fighting this terrible drug trade. Many source-country governments face major threats to their democratic institutions from drug violence and corruption. Finally, all of us face a terrible threat from billions of dollars in illegal funds that distort our economic development and assault the integrity of our banking systems.

The time has come for all of us, as responsible governments, to understand that the world community cannot allow international criminal organizations to gain a foothold in any country

The United States government is absolutely committed to helping all nations achieve full compliance with the goals and objectives set forth by the United Nations in its 1988 Convention. We will support regional and sub-regional efforts to address drug production, trafficking, and consumption. We will share information with our partners. We are prepared to assist in institution-building so that judiciaries, legislatures, and law-enforcement agencies successfully can counter international traffickers. We will support an international effort to stop money laundering. The magnitude of drug profits that filter through international financial institutions makes them conspicuous. Such sums are difficult to conceal from attentive bankers and governments working together. The U.S. government will continue working with our hemispheric partners to develop means of identifying and seizing illegal drug proceeds as they pass through banking systems.

The drug problem is a shared agony throughout this hemisphere. It affects us all differently. In the United States, drug abuse has enormous health consequences and also generates violent crime and unsafe streets. In Mexico, the problem is different. Geography and a common two-thousand-mile border have drawn international drug trafficking organizations to that country as a route to the United States. In the Caribbean, small island nations with constrained resources have difficulty protecting their extensive coast lines. Cooperative action holds the promise of reducing trafficking through this transit zone. In Colombia and Peru, drug cultivation and production now provide resources to narcoguerrilla organizations. While the drug-abuse menace is a common problem for us all, it takes on different forms. All of us must guard against allowing drug-trafficking organizations from gaining a stranglehold on our economies, our families, or our democratic processes.

We are confident that we can continue making significant progress in the Western Hemisphere against drug production and trafficking. The U.S. 1997 National Drug Control Strategy affirms our commitment to helping reduce the availability of cocaine. We identify as a top international drug-policy priority support for the efforts of Bolivia, Colombia, and Peru in reducing coca cultivation. We are in the process of developing a regional initiative, the goal of which is nothing less than complete elimination within the next decade of coca destined for illicit cocaine production. The success of Peruvian drug-control efforts in reducing coca cultivation by eighteen percent in 1996 and 1997 causes us to feel optimistic about our ability to achieve cooperatively this ambitious objective.

Government Cooperation Can Combat Drug Trafficking

by the National Governors' Association

About the author: *The National Governors' Association strives to support the work of the governors by providing a bipartisan forum to help shape national policy and to solve state problems.*

To reduce the presence of illegal drugs, drug-related organized crime, and the adverse effects of drug and alcohol abuse in society requires a comprehensive strategy involving federal, state, and local governments. This approach should include international cooperation, diplomatic initiatives, drug law enforcement, education, prevention, detoxification, client-based human services, treatment, and research.

States have devoted substantial resources toward reducing the demand for drugs and increasing the availability of treatment and testing. Treatment, prevention, and abstinence-based education are working, and the federal government should assist the states in their efforts to provide the services and programs needed to reduce drug demand. The Governors believe that one of the most severe public health threats is the recent rise in substance abuse among children. Youth substance abuse exacerbates juvenile crime rates and fosters low educational achievement.

The Federal Role

The federal government should accelerate resource assistance to aid in the implementation of statewide demand reduction campaigns. The profits from illicit drug trafficking can be effectively used to help state efforts to dry up the demand for these drugs.

The nation's Governors urge the President and Congress to fully fund drug and alcohol abuse education, drug courts, treatment, prevention, and law en-

Excerpted from *HR-13: Combating and Controlling Substance Abuse and Illegal Drug Trafficking Policy*, a position paper from the National Governors' Association, 2000. Reprinted with permission.

forcement efforts, including the initiative to combat and clean up methamphetamine production laboratories, at the state and local levels of government. It is through resource assistance that the federal government intends to follow through on its commitment to assist state and local governments in ridding the nation of the scourge of drugs. The Governors support additional federal resources for effective state and local treatment and prevention programs that show great promise in reducing drug trafficking and crime by forthrightly attacking the link between substance abuse and crime.

The Governors recognize that combating youth substance abuse requires the participation of all levels of government and all segments of society, especially parents. On the federal level, the federal government's interdiction and law enforcement efforts can discourage illegal drug use by youth. The federal government can also help reduce youth substance abuse through continued support for substance abuse prevention, recovery, and research programs as well as by continuing to improve the tools that measure substance abuse levels. . . .

Intensified Eradication and Interdiction

The federal government has exclusive responsibility for coordinating interdiction of drug shipments from foreign countries and assisting those countries in the eradication of drugs at the source. This should be a top priority of the federal government.

Federal funding for use of the National Guard in drug and border enforcement deserves continued support. Without the continued support of Congress and the Administration for National Guard counterdrug activities, the Guard will not be able to provide assistance to state and local law enforcement. Annual budget fluctuations prevent the counterdrug program from attracting and maintaining needed personnel and support, causing career instability with the loss of highly qualified and experienced counterdrug personnel. The Governors urge the President and Congress to ensure that the process for approving state plans for National Guard drug interdiction efforts is streamlined to ensure that available

> *"Youth substance abuse exacerbates juvenile crime rates and fosters low educational achievement."*

funds are distributed to states as expeditiously as possible following submission of a plan to the National Guard Bureau.

The military should work with federal, state, and local officials in multigovernmental efforts to control drug smuggling into the country and drug-related organized crime. The Governors urge the President and Congress to utilize the role of U.S. military forces in interdiction efforts. This role should cover all regions of the country and can be fostered through more frequent joint military and law enforcement missions and compacts promoting intergovernmental cooperation. . . .

The Federal Role in Reducing International Drug Trafficking

Although the nation's Governors continue to combat the supply and demand for drugs through public awareness campaigns and increased funding for antidrug programs in education, prevention, treatment, and law enforcement, international drug trafficking continues to flourish and expand its global impact. Drug interdiction must be addressed in an international context and must be considered a crucial element of foreign policy. Therefore, the U.S. State Department, the U.S. Agency for International Development, and the Drug Enforcement Administration's foreign antidrug operation must be given sufficient resources to be effective.

> *"The military should work with federal, state, and local officials in multigovernmental efforts to control drug smuggling into the country and drug-related organized crime."*

The Governors support increased federal action against the efforts of the international drug cartels to expand their markets and their drug operations into other countries. Success requires the full cooperation of all governments that struggle with international drug traffickers and cartels within their borders. Therefore, the nation's Governors urge the Administration and Congress to significantly tighten procedures for certifying foreign countries for eligibility to receive U.S. aid based on their cooperation with U.S. surveillance, interdiction, and eradication efforts. The Governors particularly encourage the federal government to continue monitoring the ties of host nation officials to drug trafficking organizations as a key factor in determining whether the President should decertify [or withdraw international assistance from] a potentially offending state. In addition, in cases where the amount of U.S. aid to some uncooperative countries is inconsequential, the federal government should develop other sanctions against those countries whose governments participate in, benefit from, or fail to combat international drug trafficking.

Drug Legalization

The nation's Governors are strongly opposed to the legalization of illicit drugs. The laws of our country are a statement of a culture's ethos. In this case, laws are firm reminders of the devastating impact illicit drugs have on young people, families, and entire communities. More important, legalization would serve to reverse the gains made by a number of states to reduce illicit drug use through education, treatment, and prevention. For these reasons, the nation's Governors believe illicit drug legalization is not a viable alternative, either as a philosophy or as a practical reality.

Certification Laws Can Combat Drug Trafficking

by Jeane Kirkpatrick

About the author: *Jeane Kirkpatrick served as ambassador to the United Nations under Ronald Reagan. She is currently a law professor at Georgetown University and a senior fellow at the American Enterprise Institute.*

I believe that drug certification and our drug certification program [which denies U.S. aid to countries the president deems noncomplicit in the war on drugs] is based on the undoubted facts that the overwhelming majority of American people desire to combat the scourge of drugs, that they desire their government to do everything that is possible and feasible to keep drugs out of the country, off the streets, and that they desire to deal with it at every level that is possible and feasible.

We know that it is possible to affect the amount of drugs headed for the United States and arriving in the United States. We know that was proved beyond reasonable doubt in both the Ronald Reagan and the George Bush Administrations, when monthly use of cocaine was reduced by 80 percent. The certification program, it was generally believed by students of the problem, made a major contribution to this success.

There is no question that Americans desire to wage and win this war on drugs. No question that three quarters of Americans desire to make foreign aid contingent on countries' cooperation with the United States in the war on drugs. The drug war, as the majority of Americans understand, not only brings drugs, but it also brings crime and terrorism and a variety of problems to our country and our streets.

Taxpayers' Money

I believe it makes no sense at all [for] the U.S. Government to give taxpayer money to countries that do not cooperate with the United States in the pursuit of major objectives which are of broad concern to the American people. To give

Excerpted from Jeane Kirkpatrick's testimony before the U.S. House of Representatives Committee on International Relations, April 29, 1998.

foreign aid to countries whose governments are passive in the war against drug dealers, when those drug dealers export their poisons to American streets, simply tells that government and the world, in my judgment, that the United States is not really serious when it urges action against the international drug traders. Just as giving aid to countries that violate human rights, with serious violations of human rights of their own citizens, testifies that we are not really serious about those human rights violations and those practices. No foreign country which engages in the drug trade and declines to cooperate with the United States in suppressing the drug trade, I believe, has a right to receive foreign aid from the United States. They do not have a right to receive foreign aid from us, and American taxpayers have a right not to have our taxes distributed to those who acquiesce in the violation of our laws and our values.

The fact that certification is not wholly successful, the fact that certification does not wholly solve the problem is assuredly no reason to abandon it—any more than we would abandon a medicine that did not wholly eliminate a disease. Neither should we abandon certification because some foreign government might be offended by it—or indeed, is offended by it, or embarrassed by it. The fact is that our foreign policy should be designed and implemented to serve the most basic values and goals of the American people. The American people should be offended by the failure of their government to take full account of their views and values in the implementation of our laws and the design of our policies.

U.S. Interests

During the Reagan Administration, the United States adopted a policy of linking U.S. foreign assistance with the manner in which the recipient countries treated our most basic interests and values. At the United Nations, for example, we made it a point to inform other governments about those very few issues in which there were significant U.S. interests and stakes. If another government deliberately opposed those serious interests and values, we took that into account—and gave advanced notice that we would take it into account—in deciding whether or not to grant aid in the coming year. There were few instances in which aid was, in fact, reduced. But in those few instances, there was a visible, marked improvement in the behavior of the countries, subsequently. In a few cases—a very few cases—the flow of U.S. aid was entirely eliminated. I do not forget that an ambassador of an African country

> *"Three quarters of Americans desire to make foreign aid contingent on countries' cooperation with the United States in the war on drugs."*

with a decent government said to me on one occasion after his country had had his foreign aid from the United States reduced, a policy of deliberate continuous neglect of U.S. interests—important U.S. interests, not trivial U.S. interests and values—said to me, "'we really never knew you really cared about that issue." That's a comment that I do not forget. This was a very intelligent African ambassador. And he said, "now we know you really care."

I know that it is often said that such policies and such an approach damages our relations with other countries. I believe that policies which seriously violate and damage American values and interests damage their relations with the United States, and should damage their relations with the United States if they are pursuing

> *"Our foreign policy should be designed and implemented to serve the most basic values and goals of the American people."*

policies which break our laws, seduce our youth, and introduce crime to our streets. I read the report in which Rand Beers, the Acting Assistant Secretary of State for the Bureau of Narcotics and Law Enforcement Affairs, said of certification, "it is policy that is controversial not because it has failed but because it is working." Not popular, but working. He has also emphasized that it is the law of the land.

There is a statutory requirement that that policy be enforced. Certification is an imperfect tool with which our government seeks to serve deeply held values, strongly held desires of the American people—a great majority of the American people. It is not an exercise in traditional diplomacy any more than concern with human rights is an exercise in traditional diplomacy. Interestingly enough, many of the same people who oppose drug certification also oppose taking account of human rights practices and violations in the conduct of our foreign policy. . . .

Certification Laws Reflect American Values

In giving a role to the Congress, the Constitution makes entirely clear that foreign, as well as domestic, policy should be responsive to the people—to Americans, to ordinary Americans. It may be true that the certification process communicates distrust and breeds hard feelings. It also gets attention and forces other governments to take account of our needs as a price of our support. That's, I think, not unreasonable.

U.S. economic and military assistance is not equally available to all countries. It is and should be available to those countries to whom we are related by mutual respect and mutual regard. Certification seems to me to be one means, and until we get something better, an important means for ensuring that this will be the case. Obviously, a drug certification program does not solve the drug problem. That's perfectly clear. But our drug certification program, as I understand it, does, in fact, reflect a realistic understanding of the limited powers of other governments in some cases to deal with the problems themselves and it provides assistance in some cases, and does not hold governments responsible for doing things which they cannot do—for controlling sectors in their own society which they cannot control. But it offers help. It asks for cooperation and effort.

Human Rights Violations

When we look at the list of countries that were in 1997 decertified for assistance, it's striking—Afghanistan, Burma, Colombia—maybe there's a question about Colombia—Iran, Nigeria, Syria. All of these, interestingly enough, are—or almost all are—countries that are also our short list for the systematic and continuing violation of the basic human rights of their own people.

I believe that this is no accident; that the drug trade thrives in countries with repressive governments which do not respect the rights of their own people. It thrives in countries which do not feature a rule of law; which are governed by violent dictators. It thrives in countries in which there is little regard for any American values, including certainly the promotion of the drug trade. I believe that insofar as the drug decertification program fails to achieve its goals, then the challenge to the Congress is to improve it. The challenge to the Congress is not, in fact, to abandon it—and in favor of some multinational effort over which we would have little control and over whose standards we would also have very limited influence.

If the process does not move us toward the goals, then the Congress should improve it. The alternative to an imperfect policy, in my opinion, should be a better program. It should not be the abandonment of any effort to achieve those goals.

I have a longstanding concern for U.S. relations with other countries in this hemisphere, and that concern remains very strong for me. I believe, in thinking about the countries and the drug decertification and certification, and so forth, it is important to bear in mind that this is not simply a hemispheric problem, but a global problem. We have not only problems with countries in this hemisphere but also countries elsewhere in the world. And I believe that any action by this Committee should take all those into account and should take as its goal the improvement of this unquestionably imperfect instrument.

Development Programs Can Combat Drug Trafficking

by Anja Korenblik

About the author: *Anja Korenblik works with the Supply Reduction and Law Enforcement Section of the United Nations International Drug Control Programme.*

Confronting the illicit trade in drugs and its effects remains a major challenge for the international community. As the organization responsible for leading United Nations' action against the global drug problem, the United Nations Drug Control Programme (UNDCP) tries to identify, understand and contain the forces which lead individuals to resort to illicit drug production, trafficking and abuse.

The illicit cultivation of opium poppy and coca is directly linked to rural poverty. The reduction of rural poverty—particularly through sustainable natural resource management—is therefore a necessary component of UNDCP supply reduction programmes. So called Alternative Development Programmes aim to reduce and eliminate the illicit cultivation of drug crops through development measures which are often more sustainable, more promising and more readily accepted than strategies based on repression only.

Over the last twenty-five years, UNDCP has actively promoted and supported international efforts to reduce illicit cultivation of opium poppy in South East and South West Asia. Twelve years ago, a similar action was launched in the Andean Sub-region in respect of coca cultivation. In the course of those years UNDCP's approach in the field has substantially improved. The crop substitution projects of the early 1970s which focussed on direct replacement of illicit crops by licit ones, have lead to refinement and improvement of the approach applied.

Alternative Development programmes now aim at the elimination or prevention of the production of illicit crops through a methodology encompassing a broader concept of rural development aimed at improving the overall quality of

Reprinted, with permission, from "Alternative Development: Drug Control Through Rural Development," by Anja Korenblik, posted February 28, 1999, on the website of the ACC Network on Rural Development and Food Security at www.accnetwork.net/en/themes/ACCt4.htm.

life of the target population by addressing not only income but also education, health, infrastructure and social services.

Dangerous Crops

UNDCP estimates that the global area devoted to illicit opium poppy cultivation was about 280,000 hectares (ha) in 1996, with 90 per cent of illicit cultivation taking place in Afghanistan and Myanmar. Most of the world's coca is grown in the Andean countries (220,000 ha): Bolivia, Colombia and Peru together account for more than 98 per cent of the world cocaine supplies. Altogether about 700,000 families, or around 4 million people, depend on income derived from the cultivation of coca bush and opium poppy. Most of these people live below the poverty line and receive on average 50 per cent of their income from this activity. Although the drug trade often helps them cope with food shortages and the vagaries of other agricultural markets, economic dependence on illicit crops is not sustainable in the long run. Forming an enclave in the national economy and excluded from mainstream development, the cultivation of coca bush and opium poppy leaves farmers in the hands of ruthless and unreliable middlemen. Also, there is always the threat of forced eradication of their illicit crop by the Government. In some countries, such as Colombia, many have become mere employees in large commercial farms owned by traffickers of narcotic drugs. Most of the 700,000 families, given suitable alternatives, would gladly switch to other sources of income.

"The illicit cultivation of opium poppy and coca is directly linked to rural poverty."

The commonalities of communities with illicit cultivation across the regions lie in the fact that they live in remote, often backward areas, and in subsistence economies where cash and credit needs are met by the opium/coca crop. In order to reach these remote groups through project interventions, and to induce the cultivators to change the agricultural production system as well as their household planning and survival strategies, any intervention will have to be tailored to the specific needs of the local population with its specific characteristics. Gradual reduction of illicit cultivation over a period of several years (6–10) in accordance with locally determined rural development plans, within realistic time frames, are essential elements for drug control interventions in such areas. Sustainability of these interventions should be achieved through a systematically applied participatory approach.

Ideal conditions for Alternative Development include:

- Effective control of the area by central government and an absence of counter pressure from insurgent groups.
- The provision of an enabling, sustainable economic environment at the national and international level which facilitates the presence of market forces that make illicit cultivation less attractive.

- Consistently applied disincentives through law enforcement and crop eradication.

However, these conditions are often not fulfilled and efforts for Alternative Development—narrowly or broadly targeted—need to include measures to build up these prerequisites.

Methodology

During the last ten years of investment in Alternative Development, a methodology of project design, planning and implementation has been developed. The three most important developments are:

i. Community participation: Emphasis is placed on community-based approaches to natural resource management in sustainable production systems. Such an approach is consistent with participatory, people-centered methods of development that rely on local people's knowledge, skills, interests and needs as a basis for appropriate interventions. This approach is especially important for Alternative Development given the socio-cultural dimensions of illicit drug-crop cultivation.

ii. Institution building: Institution building at all levels of project design, planning and implementation is necessary to the development of sustainable local institutions through community development approaches. A parallel supporting measure is institution building specifically for drug control by providing support and technical advisory services to governments.

iii. Constant monitoring and evaluation: All Alternative Development projects need to make provisions for data collection and monitoring of trends in respect of illicit crop reduction and improvement of education, health, infrastructure and social services. Regular analysis of data should provide lessons to be shared, permit adjustments and facilitate the identification of those intervention models which can be sustained and which should be replicated on a larger scale.

Alternative Development programmes can be targeted to cultivation areas only or can be more broadly targeted, trying to improve growth in outputs and jobs, nation- or even region-wide. A combination of the two has proved to be most successful, because the application of generalized development assistance to non-growing areas mitigates the risk of displacing cultivation

"In some countries . . . many [farmers] have become mere employees in large commercial farms owned by traffickers of narcotic drugs."

to near-by areas with similar social, economic and agricultural characteristics. UNDCP has demonstrated that narrowly targeted Alternative Development programmes can be successful in the immediate area of intervention. For example, in project areas in Peru, coca cultivation has been reduced by 95 per cent and in the Dir district of Pakistan, poppy cultivation may soon disappear. In Thailand, Alternative Development measures have led to virtual elimination of opium poppy cultivation. However, it has been argued that the excellent results achieved in countries such as Pakistan and Thailand were greatly facilitated by the displacement of cultivation into neighboring Afghanistan and Myanmar (the "balloon effect"). Therefore, Alternative Development today, while still focussing on major illicit cultivation areas, recognizes the importance of a broader approach, tackling several cultivation areas while at the same time monitoring the areas where new cultivation could start.

More Effort Is Needed

Global investment into Alternative Development measures over the last ten years has amounted to $718 million, of which UNDCP provided 36 per cent and other sources, mostly bilateral, provided 64 per cent. With an annual investment of approximately $70 million globally, the total investment to control and eliminate production of illicit cultivation has been relatively small. Also, the areas covered by Alternative Development programmes are only a small part of the total area under illicit cultivation. For example in Peru, the country with the largest coca growing areas, only approximately 10 per cent of the area under cultivation is covered by UNDCP-supported Alternative Development projects.

"Development programmes can be successful in the immediate area of intervention."

The above confirms the pioneering role of UNDCP, contained in the selection of investment programmes in some of the most remote and difficult areas, which are often avoided by other multilateral, bilateral and private investors. The opening up of these areas with initial investment, however limited, and the attempts to link such areas to national mainstream economic development has been a major achievement of Alternative Development interventions. However, the sustainability of Alternative Development depends essentially on whether and how farmers capitalize on the economic alternatives made available to them. Alternative Development must have two pillars as its foundation: national drug control plans and agricultural development plans. The long-term sustainability of illicit crop reduction and elimination is inextricably linked to agricultural development. Progress in reducing illicit supply will depend not only on the political commitment to drug control but also on Government efforts to provide and or nurture genuine alternatives and additional off-farm income opportunities.

At present, UNDCP is moving towards a global approach to Alternative Development. There is sufficient evidence to conclude at this point in time that Alternative Development can indeed be successful: the methodology has been developed, experiences and knowledge have accumulated and successes in project areas have been achieved. Future Alternative Development projects will need to involve active partnerships with Governments to a greater extent than in the past, making a move away from the benefactor/recipient model that has been the basis for many previous programmes. UNDCP's role will involve a greater element of advice to the Government, mobilizing political support and facilitating bilateral and multilateral funding. At the Special Session of the General Assembly in 1998, a first step was taken when governments reaffirmed their strong support to UNDCP's work in Alternative Development. . . .

With the broad membership including Government, civil society, private sector, donors and UN organizations, an appropriate combination of political and civil society commitment and financial resources could be obtained for the implementation of Alternative Development projects with the reduction in supply as one important outcome.

Reducing American Demand Can Combat Drug Trafficking

by Jac Wilder VerSteeg

About the author: *Jac Wilder VerSteeg is an editorial writer for the* Palm Beach Post *in Florida.*

In August 1999, paramilitary soldiers in Colombia killed 13 people, including a 13-year-old girl, and dumped their bodies by the side of the road—a warning to villagers suspected of dealings with communist rebels. That massacre brought the number of civilians killed in 1999 in Colombia to nearly 850.

For those Americans who use cocaine or heroin, the line between their drug abuse and those murders is not as blurry as they might pretend.

The money Americans spend on drugs finances killers on all sides of Colombia's civil war, which has killed 35,000 people during the past decade. Combatants' total drug profits, exact amount unknown for obvious reasons, is estimated at between $500 million and $1 billion annually.

There is a European market, and even a small but growing domestic drug market in the principal drug countries of Colombia, Peru, Venezuela, Ecuador and Bolivia. But the real blood money comes from American pockets.

It comes in two ways, actually. There's the cash yuppies snort up their noses, and there's the money—$289 million in 1999—the United States sends to Colombia in anti-drug aid.

The Bill Clinton administration declared Colombia's precarious political condition an emergency and reiterated its commitment to combat drugs on two fronts. But don't look for good news on either. There's a bloated bureaucratic plan for reducing demand in the U.S. and a billion-dollar plan for crippling drug production in Colombia and surrounding countries.

Colombians and others in Latin America are tired of U.S. hypocrisy and hammer at a simple, embarrassing fact: Without the U.S. market, the drug trade

Excerpted from "Colombia Dies for America's Highs," by Jac Wilder VerSteeg, *Palm Beach (Florida) Post*, August 29, 1999. Reprinted with permission.

would wither on its own. And behind all the hype about [then] drug-policy czar General Barry McCaffrey's plan to cut U.S. demand, there is another embarrassing fact: The plan is not designed to provide specific, verifiable progress on reducing demand in the United States until 2002—long after everyone who set the goals has faded from the scene.

The United States Promotes Drug Trafficking

It's fairly easy to see how the money Americans spend on their cocaine and heroin highs feeds Colombia's drug trade. But how does U.S. anti-drug aid end up promoting *drug* trafficking instead?

In many ways, the drug-fighting money we send to Colombia does exactly what it's supposed to do. Colombian police, whom U.S. advisers train, fly on U.S. planes to spray poison on coca and poppy plants that U.S. surveillance technology spots. Eradicating drug crops or otherwise cutting off the production end is a proven method—trafficking plummeted in Peru when President Alberto Fujimori let his air force shoot down planes suspected of running drugs.

Colombia has not made that kind of progress. Rebels belonging to two groups, the Revolutionary Armed Forces of Colombia (FARC), with about 15,000 members, and the National Liberation Army (ELN), with about 5,000, make millions to finance their war by selling protection to drug producers. The intertwined interests of drug traffickers and rebels guarantees U.S. anti-drug aid has a political component. When we spend money to wipe out drug protection, we also spend money to wipe out rebels trying to take over the government of President Andres Pastrana. To many, this is a repeat of this century's major theme in Latin America: The United States supports right-wing factions that commit atrocities in the name of fighting communism.

If the leftist rebels were the only group protecting drug producers, the United States and Colombian government would have nothing to answer for. But right-wing paramilitary forces, loosely allied with the government in fighting against the rebels, also drag in drug money. The paramilitaries have not been targeted to the same extent. In fact, the government and United States are accused of winking at the paramilitaries. In some cases, army units may have disguised themselves as paramilitary forces and massacred civilians. Such human rights abuses led to U.S. decisions to cut off the army from most aid, which flowed instead to the less corrupted, more modern police force. But the atrocities create support for the rebels,

> *"The real blood money comes from American pockets."*

which in turn perpetuates and even accelerates the drug trade.

In congressional testimony in August 1999, General McCaffrey tried to downplay fears that U.S. aid to Colombia has become less an anti-drug effort and more a military operation to defeat the rebels. "We are determined to help reestablish the rule of law and allow the development of legitimate economic alternatives to the drug trade," General McCaffrey said. "Such support will be limited to counter drug training, resources, equipment, intelligence and regional political support operations as U.S. policy is absolutely to not intervene militarily in Colombia's internal struggle."

Read that list again. Equipment, resources, intelligence, political support. How is the U.S. not intervening? And if the U.S. were not involved militarily, General McCaffrey would not have had to issue this statement in July 1999:

"Our thoughts and prayers are with the families of the five brave U.S. Army aviators and their two Colombian air force comrades who lost their lives in a fatal air crash in southern Colombia while on a counter-drug mission."

It is not surprising that General McCaffrey, a Vietnam and Desert Storm veteran and former commander of the U.S. Southern Command in Panama, would lean toward military action—particularly now that rebels have broken their promise to negotiate peace with President Pastrana. The problem, as always, is knowing where to draw the line. In 1999 there were roughly 200 U.S. military personnel in Colombia, along with an unknown number of agents from the CIA and Drug Enforcement Administration. Still, General McCaffrey also is not exaggerating the American interest in halting drug traffic from Colombia, which supplies an estimated 80 percent of this country's cocaine and 75 percent of its heroin. But history indicates that if America stops drug traffic in one spot, it bulges to another—so long as there is a demand. In fact, Colombia's recent increase in drug involvement stems in part from two successes.

> "*Without the U.S. market, the drug trade would wither on its own.*"

When Peru broke the chain of drug trafficking there (a success which, unfortunately, proved to be temporary), the activity moved to Colombia. And though the Colombian government smashed the Cali and Medellin drug cartels in the past several years, smaller and more independent producers that filled the vacuum have been harder to trace and target. . . .

Reducing the Demand for Drugs

The ultimate goal, as General McCaffrey acknowledges, is eliminating U.S. demand for the drugs. Indeed, that demand has declined considerably since 1979, when a survey found 14 percent of people 12 and older had used illegal drugs in the previous month. The figure now is roughly 6 percent. But most of that decline came in the late 1980s. Overall, drug use has been steady during the 1990s and has not declined significantly since General McCaffrey's appointment in 1996. Heroin use, negligible as the 1990s began, has increased in recent years. More people now seek treatment for heroin addiction than for cocaine addiction.

[One] recent survey, released in August 1999, found declining drug use by children 12 to 17—a drop to 9.9 percent from 11.4 percent, which Gen. Mc-

Caffrey said shows that "America's team effort is working." But an increase among young adults 18 to 25—to 16.1 percent from 14.7 percent—negated that decline and left overall illicit drug use at 6.2 percent or 13.6 million people. Those stagnant numbers raise doubts about General McCaffrey's ambitious goal to cut the U.S. demand for illegal drugs. Using 1996 statistics as a baseline, his agency's target is a 25 percent reduction by 2002 and a 50 percent reduction by 2007. The dates involved suggest a different drug czar will be in office before the accountability becomes real. . . .

> *"The ultimate goal . . . is eliminating U.S. demand for the drugs."*

General McCaffrey or any director of the Office of Drug Control Policy has an impossible task. Try coordinating the Army, Drug Enforcement Administration, FBI, CIA, police departments from Miami to New York to Dallas to Los Angeles and federal and state addiction prevention services—to name a few. Add to that the necessity of working with foreign governments, armies and police forces.

The opponents are rich and ruthless. And the administration's goals and programs are fodder for political debate. When U.S. Representative John Mica, (R-Winter Park), held hearings in 1999 on the Colombian emergency, he declared: "While the (Bill Clinton) administration grasps for effective policy to deal with this emergency, Colombia's narco-terrorism now poses the single greatest threat to the stability of our hemisphere."

Representative Mica is too simple in assigning blame. Republicans have had their own misadventures in Latin America, most recently the Iran-Contra scandal of the Ronald Reagan and George Bush administrations. And all those previous Latin American disasters have helped create the problems that General McCaffrey faces.

Representative Mica, however, isn't far off in his assessment of the threat. The real source of that threat isn't the communist rebels or the drug producers or the brutal paramilitaries or inept Latin American leaders or America's bureaucratic drug warriors. It isn't even the hard-core addict.

The final source, the one who pays for the planes and boats and bullets, smugly treats himself to a "recreational" high.

Law Enforcement Cannot Combat Drug Trafficking

by Joseph McNamara

About the author: *Joseph McNamara is a former police chief and has written four books on policing.*

"It's the money, stupid." After 35 years as a police officer in three of the country's largest cities, that is my message to the righteous politicians who obstinately proclaim that a war on drugs will lead to a drug-free America. About $500 worth of heroin or cocaine in a source country will bring in as much as $100,000 on the streets of an American city. All the cops, armies, prisons, and executions in the world cannot impede a market with that kind of tax-free profit margin. It is the illegality that permits the obscene markup, enriching drug traffickers, distributors, dealers, crooked cops, lawyers, judges, politicians, bankers, and businessmen.

Naturally, these people are against reform of the drug laws. Drug crooks align themselves with their avowed enemies, such as the Drug Enforcement Administration, in opposing drug reform. They are joined by many others with vested economic interests. President Eisenhower warned of a military–industrial complex that would elevate the defense budget unnecessarily. That military–industrial complex pales in comparison to the host of industries catering to our national puritanical hypocrisy—researchers willing to tell the government what it wants to hear, prison builders, correction and parole officers' associations, drug-testing companies, and dubious purveyors of anti-drug education. . . .

Sadly, the police have been pushed into a war they did not start and cannot win. It was not the police who lobbied in 1914 for passage of the Harrison Act, which first criminalized drugs. It was the Protestant missionary societies in China, the Woman's Christian Temperance Union, and other such organizations that viewed the taking of psychoactive substances as sinful. These groups gradually got their religious tenets enacted into penal statutes under which the "sinners" go to jail. The religious origin is significant for two reasons. If drugs had

Excerpted from "The War on Drugs Is Lost," by Joseph McNamara, *National Review*, February 12, 1996. Copyright © 1996 by National Review, Inc., 215 Lexington Ave., New York, NY 10016. Reprinted with permission.

been outlawed because the police had complained that drug use caused crime and disorder, the policy would have been more acceptable to the public and won more compliance. And the conviction that the use of certain drugs is immoral chills the ability to scrutinize rationally and to debate the effects of the drug war. When Ethan Nadelmann, director of the Lindesmith Center, pointed out once that it was illogical for the most hazardous drugs, alcohol and nicotine, to be legal while less dangerous drugs were illegal, he was roundly denounced. A leading conservative supporter of the drug war contended that while alcohol and nicotine addiction was unhealthy and could even cost lives, addiction to illegal drugs could result in the loss of one's soul. No empirical proof was given.

The demonizing of these drugs and their users encourages demagoguery. William Bennett, the nation's first drug czar, would cut off the heads of drug sellers. Bennett's anti-drug rhetoric is echoed by Joseph Califano, the liberal former Secretary of Health, Education, and Welfare, [and] chairman of the Center on Addiction and Substance Abuse at Columbia University. In June 1995, the Center hysterically suggested (with great media coverage) that binge drinking and other substance abuse were taking over the nation's colleges, leading to an increase in rapes, assaults, and murders and to the spread of AIDS and other sexually transmitted diseases. The validity of the research in Califano's report was persuasively debunked by Kathy McNamara-Meis, writing in *Forbes Media Critic*. She was equally critical of the media for accepting the Center's sensational statements.

Examining Alternative Policies

Conservatives like Bennett normally advocate minimal government. Liberals like Califano ordinarily recoil from the draconian prison sentences and property seizures used in the drug war. This illustrates why it is so difficult to get politicians to concede that alternative approaches to drug control need to be studied. We are familiar with the perception that the first casualty in any war is truth. Eighty years of drug-war propaganda has so influenced public opinion that most politicians believe they will lose their jobs if their opponents can claim they are soft on drugs and crime. Yet, public doubt is growing. Gallup reports that in 1990 only 4 percent of Americans believed that "arresting the people who use drugs" is the best way for the government to allocate resources.

"It is the illegality that permits the obscene markup, enriching drug traffickers, distributors, dealers, crooked cops, lawyers, judges, politicians, bankers, and businessmen."

It was my own experience as a policeman trying to enforce the laws against drugs that led me to change my attitude about drug-control policy. The analogy to the Vietnam War is fitting. I was a willing foot soldier at the start of the modern drug war, pounding a beat in Harlem. During the early 1960s, as heroin use spread, we made many arrests, but it did not take long before cops realized that arrests did not lessen drug selling or drug use.

I came to realize just how ineffective we were in deterring drug use one day when my partner and I arrested an addict for possession of a hypodermic needle and heroin. Our prisoner had already shot up, but the heroin charge we were prepared to level at him was based on the tiny residue in the bottle cap used to heat the fix. It was petty, but then—and now—such arrests are valued because they can be used to claim success, like the body counts during the Vietnam War.

> *"In 1990 only 4 percent of Americans believed that 'arresting the people who use drugs' is the best way for the government to allocate resources."*

In this case the addict offered to "give" us a pusher in exchange for letting him go. He would lure the pusher into a hallway where we could then arrest him in the act of selling drugs. We trailed the addict along Lenox Avenue. To our surprise, he spoke to one man after another.

It suddenly struck me as humiliating, the whole scene. Here it was, broad daylight. We were brilliantly visible, in uniform, in a marked police car. and yet a few feet away, our quarry was attempting one drug transaction after another. The first two dealers weren't deterred by our presence—they were simply sold out, and we could not arrest them without the goods. We finally arrested the third pusher, letting the first addict escape, as we had covenanted. The man we brought in was selling drugs only to support his own habit.

Questionable Ethics

Another inherent difficulty in drug enforcement is that violators are engaging in consensual activity and seek privacy. Every day, millions of drug crimes similar to what took place in front of our police car occur without police knowledge. To enforce drug laws the police have to resort to undercover work, which is dangerous to them and also to innocent bystanders. Drug enforcement often involves questionable ethical behavior by the police, such as what we did in letting a guilty person go free because he enticed someone else into violating the law.

Soldiers in a war need to dehumanize the enemy, and many cops look on drug users as less than human. The former police chief of Los Angeles, Daryl Gates, testified before the United States Senate that casual users should be taken out and shot. He defended the statement to the *Los Angeles Times* by saying, "We're in a war." New York police officers convicted of beating and robbing drug dealers . . . rationalized their crimes by saying it was impossible to stop drug dealing and these guys were the enemy. Why should they get to keep all the money?

Police scandals are an untallied cost of the drug war. The FBI, the Drug Enforcement Administration (DEA), and even the Coast Guard have had to admit to corruption. The gravity of the police crimes is as disturbing as the volume. In New Orleans, a uniformed cop in league with a drug dealer has been convicted of murdering her partner and shop owners during a robbery committed while she was on patrol. In Washington, D.C., and in Atlanta, cops in drug stings were arrested for stealing and taking bribes. New York State troopers falsified drug evidence that sent people to prison.

And it is not just the rank and file. The former police chief of Detroit went to prison for stealing police drug-buy money. In a small New England town, the chief stole drugs from the evidence locker for his own use. And the DEA agent who arrested Panama's General Manuel Noriega is in jail for stealing laundered drug money.

Casualties of War

The drug war is as lethal as it is corrupting. And the police and drug criminals are not the only casualties. An innocent 75-year-old African-American minister died of a heart attack struggling with Boston cops who were mistakenly arresting him because an informant had given them the wrong address. A rancher in Ventura County, California, was killed by a police SWAT team serving a search warrant in the mistaken belief that he was growing marijuana. In Los Angeles, a three-year-old girl died of gunshot wounds after her mother took a wrong turn into a street controlled by a drug-dealing gang. They fired on the car because it had invaded their marketplace.

The violence comes from the competition for illegal profits among dealers, not from crazed drug users. Professor Milton Friedman has estimated that as many as 10,000 additional homicides a year are plausibly attributed to the drug war.

Worse still, the drug war has become a race war in which non-whites are arrested and imprisoned at 4 to 5 times the rate whites are, even though most drug crimes are committed by whites. The Sentencing Research Project reports that one-third of black men are in jail or under penal supervision, largely because of drug arrests. The drug war has established thriving criminal enterprises which recruit teenagers into criminal careers.

"Drug enforcement often involves questionable ethical behavior by the police."

It was such issues that engaged law-enforcement leaders—most of them police chiefs—from fifty agencies during a two-day conference at the Hoover Institution in May 1995. Among the speakers was . . . Mayor Kurt Schmoke, who told the group that he had visited a high school and asked the students if the high dropout rate was due to kids' being hooked on drugs. He was told that the kids were dropping out because they were hooked on drug money, not drugs. He also told us that when he went to community meetings he would ask the audience three questions. 1) "Have we won the drug war?"

People laughed. 2) "Are we winning the drug war?" People shook their heads. 3) "If we keep doing what we are doing will we have won the drug war in ten years?" The answer was a resounding No.

At the end of the conference, the police participants completed an evaluation form. Ninety percent voted no confidence in the war on drugs. They were unanimous in favoring more treatment and education over more arrests and prisons. They were unanimous in recommending a presidential blue-ribbon commission to evaluate the drug war and to explore alternative methods of drug control. In sum, the tough-minded law-enforcement officials took positions directly contrary to those of Congress and the president.

One hopes that politicians will realize that no one can accuse them of being soft on drugs if they vote for changes suggested by many thoughtful people in law enforcement. If the politicians tone down their rhetoric it will permit police leaders to expose the costs of our present drug-control policies. Public opinion will then allow policy changes to decriminalize marijuana and stop the arrest of hundreds of thousands of people every year. The enormous savings can be used for what the public really wants—the prevention of violent crime.

Legalization Can Combat Drug Trafficking

by the Media Awareness Project

About the author: *The Media Awareness Project strives to influence public opinion through media coverage on public policy issues related to drugs and drug policy.*

If you say that drug prohibition is a terrible mistake and drugs should be legalized, you will hear the inevitable, and understandable, objection: "But what about the children?" Young people are vulnerable. Our laws must protect them.

We couldn't agree more. That's one major reason we think drugs should be legalized.

Legalization sounds like a strange way to protect kids from drugs, because people commonly make the mistake of thinking that a criminal ban on drugs is the highest form of drug control possible. Legalizing drugs, they believe, means surrendering control, and giving our youth easier access to substances that may harm them. In fact, exactly the opposite is true.

In the United States, the government has been surveying kids about how easy it is for them to get drugs since the 1970s. In 1979, at the height of the drug craze in the United States, 18 percent of high school seniors said it was "easy" or "fairly easy" to obtain heroin; in 1998, that figure was 35 percent. In 1998, 90 percent of high school seniors said marijuana was "easy" or "fairly easy" to get.

In 1989, when Ecstasy was still a little-known drug, 21 percent of American teens said they could get the drug with little effort; in 1998, that number was up to 38 percent.

Many may choose to ignore these numbers. After all, the American government recently announced that for the third year in a row, drug use among teenagers was down. But what the government overlooked in its press releases was that these modest declines come after years of major increases. From 1990 to 1997, the use of most drugs by young people rose alarmingly. Marijuana use hit levels not seen since the 1970s.

Reprinted, with permission, from "What About the Children?" an editorial by the Media Awareness Project published in *The Ottawa (Canada) Citizen*, September 19, 2000. Copyright 2000 The Ottawa Citizen.

Chapter 4

Lessons of Prohibition

From 1972 to 2000, the U.S. has spent spectacular amounts of money to enforce prohibition. When Ronald Reagan revved up the War on Drugs in the 1980s, the anti-drug budget was $1 billion; today, it's almost $20 billion. Despite this, American teenagers find it easier to get their hands on drugs now than ever before. Does that look like an effective way of protecting children from drugs?

Lessons can be learned from this. The reason prohibition doesn't protect kids is much the same reason it fails generally: economics. Banning drugs makes them very expensive. That makes them very profitable. That makes an unlimited number of people willing to do just about anything to sell them. And to those people, selling drugs to minors is just the same as selling to adults: illegal. The customer's age is meaningless; his cash is what matters.

So what happens when a drug is legalized? Consider alcohol. It can be sold legally to everybody but minors at legal market prices. That satisfies the demand of the overwhelming majority of consumers. As a result, there's little economic incentive for someone to risk prison by selling alcohol to minors. It's highly unlikely anyone is standing outside your teenager's school selling vodka. Marijuana, crack and Ecstasy, maybe. But not vodka.

And this situation [in Canada] exists despite the paltry efforts of governments to enforce bans on sales of legal drugs, such as alcohol, to minors. Take tobacco. The federal and provincial governments make an estimated $170 million a year on taxes from cigarettes sold illegally to minors. Governments spend just a small fraction of that on spot-checks. In Ontario, it is estimated that 115 million packs of cigarettes were sold to minors over the last five years, yet just 3,000 charges for these sales were laid. Imagine what could be accomplished if the resources devoted to busting adults who share a joint in the privacy of their own homes were, instead, used to enforce the ban on all drug sales to minors.

> *"In 1998, 90 percent of high school seniors said marijuana was 'easy' or 'fairly easy' to get."*

By criminalizing drugs, we gave up control of their sale. We handed it to biker gangs and the neighbourhood dealer—who are only too happy to sell to your teenager. By legalizing drugs, we can take that control back. If drugs are legalized, checks can be created to ensure there are no sales to minors. If drugs are one day sold in private establishments (like Holland's marijuana "coffee shops," or other private stores), tough spot-checking could easily make it in the owner's self-interest to keep minors out.

We're not deluding ourselves; determined teenagers will always be able to get their hands on things they shouldn't. But the system can be tightened to make it much more difficult. To do it, we have to take back control of the drug trade. We have to talk about legalizing drugs.

Legalization Would Not Reduce Drug Trafficking

by Carolyn C. Gargaro

About the author: *Carolyn C. Gargaro is a web designer and marketing specialist as well as a prolific writer on conservative issues.*

It seems as if the cry of "legalize drugs!" is being heard everywhere from liberals as well as conservatives. Some people argue that legalizing drugs is the only way to "win" the drug war. I agree that drug enforcement does place a burden on us. Economic resources are used up that could be used elsewhere. But the consequences of legalizing drugs would make an already large problem completely out of control. If one examines the arguments behind drug legalization, it becomes apparent that legalizing drugs won't solve any of our nation's drug problems.

I do want to clarify one thing: I will *agree* that some of the tactics being used in the drug war are ineffectual and misplaced. I often read about cases where government agents barge into an individual's house (and sometimes the wrong house!) to arrest an individual drug user whose only crime was to ingest an illegal drug, while drug lords who are bringing millions of dollars worth of drugs into our country are ignored. I believe that we need to focus more on educating children on the dangers of drugs and keeping the drug dealers from bringing the drugs into the country in the first place. I am more concerned with drug dealers who sell the drugs than the person who buys them, and I am more concerned about people who are under the influence of drugs such as PCP than those who are smoking pot in the privacy of their own home. However, just because some of the effort may be misplaced, that does not mean we should throw in the towel and make all currently illegal drugs legal. Re-focus our efforts, yes. Eliminate our efforts, no.

Taking Drugs Is an Individual's Choice

This is the main argument, especially from my fellow conservatives—that individuals have the right to do as they see fit, as long as they do not harm any-

Excerpted from "Drug Legalization?" by Carolyn C. Gargaro, published at Carolyn's Conservative Corner website, www.gargaro.com/drugs.html. Reprinted with permission.

one else. They choose to put the drugs inside their body, and they have the right to make that choice, without government interference. In theory, I understand this argument—I think there is presently too much government, and our present government limits individuals' rights too much with many inappropriate laws and regulations. But the argument regarding an individual's rights has two major flaws.

First, we don't have the right to do anything we want with our body. Can I walk down the street naked? Can I say what I want anywhere I want? (If you said "yes" to the last question, try yelling "hijack" on a plane and get back to me.) The point is, we can't do anything we want with our body. If drugs ever become legal, be prepared to see me walk around topless—after all, *men* can do it. Which is more harmful—me walking around with no shirt or me shooting up with crack? I'll be damned if people are allowed to shoot up with drugs and I have to wear a top on a blazing hot day in the summer! . . .

In addition to people not being able to do "whatever they want" with their bodies, drugs do NOT just hurt the person who chooses to use them.

For instance—I am sure people have heard about flashbacks from LSD. So, let's say people stay inside in their own home and take LSD, that can't hurt anyone, right? After all, it's in their private home, right? LSD can cause flashbacks years after taking the drug, at any time. Is that person going to have a flashback while sitting at home—or while driving? Or while operating machinery? If that person has a flashback while driving the bus and an accident results, will people be so quick to say that the bus driver's "choice" to take LSD didn't hurt anyone else?

People and their rights don't exist in a vacuum. The notion that drugs only hurt the people who use them is very shallow and illogical. One needs to look beyond themselves and look at the entire picture, and it becomes obvious that drugs have drastic effects on MANY people besides those who use them. For instance, according to a 1994 *Newsweek* report on child abuse, "Drugs now suffuse 80 percent of the caseload; sexual and physical assaults that once taxed the imagination are now common." It is also estimated that 100,000 babies a year are born addicted to cocaine. I don't think these babies chose to take these drugs.

> *"If one examines the arguments behind drug legalization, it becomes apparent that legalizing drugs won't solve any of our nation's drug problems."*

Don't tell me that drugs only hurt the user—tell that to a crack baby. Tell that to a woman who is raped by her boyfriend while he was high on PCP. Or tell that to the six-year-old that is raped by that same guy. . . . Tell that to the taxpayers who will be paying out the wazoo for higher insurance rates, more taxes for drug rehabilitation programs, and more money for court cases due to the increased number of drug related offenses.

Please don't tell me that drugs hurt only the person who chooses to use them—that's not true.

Prescription Drugs

In addition, if taking heroin or cocaine is an individual's "choice", then isn't it also their "choice" to take any other drug they wish? With this in mind, what are we going to do about all the drugs that are available by prescription only? Let's say someone wanted to take a prescription diet pill, such as "Phen-Fen" (phentermine and fenfluramine). First, one needs a prescription, and a doctor won't prescribe the drug unless he or she deems it necessary. Secondly, this drug has now been removed from the market due to dangerous side effects. However, heroin, and cocaine, for example, have dangerous side effects too. How can we prohibit drugs because of side effects and then allow people to take cocaine? If people know the side effects of a drug, isn't it their "choice" whether not to take it?

Why should I have to go to a doctor and get justification for a medication, whether it be an antibiotic or Tylenol with Codeine, when other people can take heroin whenever they choose? How are we going to justify the need for prescriptions for medications which are much less harmful when people can get crack at any time? Why can't I take a powerful prescription diet pill (I don't take these—this is an example) whenever I want, without a prescription, if people can shoot up on heroin?

> *"The notion that drugs only hurt the people who use them is very shallow and illogical."*

I can't see how we can force people to get prescriptions for other medications when they can get "hard drugs" whenever they like. So, in other words, we either have to eliminate the need for prescriptions for all drugs, and allow "banned" drugs, such as Phen-Fen, or we're going to have safer drugs harder to get than the more dangerous drugs.

Legalizing Drugs Will Mean Less Government

Strangely enough, people think that somehow the government will step aside and not be involved in the drug issue if they were legal, but that is a fantasy world. Government is all over the tobacco and alcohol industry—do people really think they won't be involved in drug regulation? Let's be realistic for a minute:

1. New laws for minors. If cigarettes and alcohol cannot be sold to minors, can anyone realistically say that drugs will not be restricted from minors? So, there will be new laws regulating the selling to minors for each and every drug that is legalized.

2. Lawsuits. I'm sure everyone is aware of all the lawsuits being brought against the tobacco industry . . . take a guess how many lawsuits will be brought up for drugs. Notice all the regulation and laws surrounding

cigarettes? Legal drugs means MORE LAWS, MORE REGULATION AND MORE GOVERNMENT, higher taxes and higher insurance rates.

3. Campaign corruption. The tobacco industry owns many politicians now—can you imagine the drug industry? We'd have politicians selling out to the drug companies instead of tobacco companies. And if one is tempted to argue that the government already is selling out to the drug lords—well, think how much that would increase if it could be done legally.

4. Do people really think that drugs will not be taxed? They will—in fact it is the tax FROM the drugs that is proposed to pay for all the new drug rehabilitation programs that will be put in place (a little more on that shortly).

Higher Taxes

Legal drugs will be regulated by the government, just as alcohol is, and thus, this government controlled item will have lots of our tax dollars poured into it. Even proponents of drug legalization, such as Nobel economist Milton Freedman and the conservative William F. Buckley admit that the government will play a significant role in legal drug regulation. Legalizing will not make us free. Instead, it will make us drones dependent on government largess for property and happiness.

Now, many say "But I don't like the government regulating other things either! I don't think they should regulate drugs or anything else!" Well, I'm certainly not one for government sticking it's nose in everywhere. If I did, I'd be a Democrat. However, legalizing drugs is NOT going to magically change the government. Legal drugs aren't going to get the government out of everything. If you want to change the government, then work on that first. Legalizing drugs will not work magic on our government—that has to be done separately. If the government is not changed prior to drug legalization, then legalized drugs will lead to more government.

Many times, when I bring up the point that increased drug use also means more tax payer funded rehabilitation programs, the response is "No, there should be no programs, they should have to pay for it themselves."

Well, wait a second . . . if this is true then the same will have to be done for people who are sick because of other self-induced problems, such as eating disorders (after all, no one is MAKING these bulimic people throw up), people with lung cancer (after all they CHOSE to smoke), people who have drinking related problems (after all, they CHOSE to drink), people with weight problems (after all they CHOSE to overeat), people with joint problems from running (they CHOSE to run) . . . do we really want that? . . .

Legalizing Drugs Will Reduce Crime

Crime will also not be reduced by drug legalization. Studies show a correlation between drug use and crime—violent crimes such as homicides, assaults and domestic violence. Why is this? It's quite simple—drugs cause violent behavior.

Has anyone considered that the reason that people committed a crime was because they were on drugs in the first place—legal or not? That they weren't necessarily committing a crime to get illegal drugs, but the drugs themselves caused a violent behavior (which would not magically go away if the drugs were legal) which lead them to committing a crime—something that would not have happened if they had not TAKEN drugs? In actuality, crime will rise when drugs are legal

> *"[Legalization] will make us drones dependent on government largess for property and happiness."*

because more people will be taking drugs. Crime is high in high-drug use areas not because people are committing a crime to get drugs, but the influence of the drugs made them more inclined to commit a crime. For instance:

- A report in the *Journal of the American Medical Association* (July 6, 1994) reports that cocaine use is linked to high rates of homicide in New York City and that "homicide victims may have provoked violence through irritability, paranoid thinking or verbal and physical aggression which are known to be pharmacologic effects of cocaine."
- Data from the National Institute of Justice (U.S. Department of Justice) Drug Use Forecasting (DUF) program underscore the crime-drugs link. Of a sample of males arrested in 23 U.S. cities in 1993, the percent testing positive for at least one drug in the DUF survey ranged from 54% in Omaha to 81% in Chicago. Among female arrestees, the percent testing positive for any drug in 20 cities ranged from 42% in San Antonio to 83% in Manhattan.

The violent behavior caused by drugs won't magically stop because the drugs are legal. Legal PCP isn't going to make a person less violent than illegally purchased PCP. So, crimes committed because of drugs will increase as the number of drug users increase with the legalization of drugs. The psychopathic behavior that drugs cause will not somehow magically stop because drugs are legal.

Legalization proponents ignore the fact that the people committing violent crimes are career criminals who will not stop their illegal activities once drugs are legalized; they will instead seek new sources of illicit revenue.

The Black Market

I am not denying that some of the present crime is due to the profit motive behind illegal drugs. I admit that causes crime. However, if drugs were legal, not only would there be an increased crime rate due to the increased number of people who were taking drugs, but there would still be a "black market" and profit motive, which brings me to my next point. The Black Market.

Many argue that the element of profit would be eliminated. If drugs were legal, it is suggested that they would be sold at regulated government stores. Or according to economist Milton Friedman, at "ordinary retail outlets." Other legalizers say that drugs would be given out to the poor addicts who could not afford them.

William F. Buckley believes prices would be low enough to wipe out the black market. Buyers would, however, be heavily taxed to pay for drug education programs and rehabilitation centers.

Yet the tax would make it possible for criminals to undercut the official price and continue to rake in profits. So then what does the government do? Make prices so low that a second-grader with a few pennies can afford it and leave them no revenue for the proposed program? And think about this: drug related crimes are the highest where crack is the cheapest.

In addition to the official price being undercut, there are drugs that even most legalizers agree are too dangerous to make legal, such as crack and PCP. So guess what! Unless we legalize crack, PCP, and heroin, the black market will still exist for the more dangerous drugs. Now, let me stress this again—even if drugs are legalized, there will still be a black market for them. I stress this because people continue to write to me wailing "But legal drugs will get rid of the black market!" The black market argument is old, unfounded, and not logical. And even if legalization eliminated the black market, does this mean we legalize everything to avoid a black market? Let's legalize stealing—after all, then these poor robbers won't have to sneak around, and possibly harm someone out of fright. See, we can cut down on deaths by legalizing robbery! Sound silly? Exactly.

Legalization Would Remove the Thrill

Past experience shows that this isn't true. Did alcohol use decrease when it was legalized? No. When abortion became legal, did abortions decrease? No. When an action becomes legal, the number of people carrying out that action increases. Drugs are not different.

In addition, unless the most harmful and addictive drugs such as crack and heroin are made legal, people will still be drawn to these "black market" drugs.

How about young children and teenagers? They won't be able to purchase drugs, just as they can't purchase alcohol. Pushers would then concentrate on young people, and how will they learn to say no to pushers when they see their parents getting high with the consent of the government? Legalization would create a large group of new drug users—children.

> *"The violent behavior caused by drugs won't magically stop because the drugs are legal."*

The drug war is long and difficult and sometimes seems hopeless but we shouldn't just give up. As William Bennett, a strong fighter in the drug war states, "Imagine if, in the darkest days of 1940, Winston Churchill had rallied the West by saying, 'This war looks hopeless, and besides, it costs too much. Hitler can't be THAT bad. Let's surrender and see what happens.'" This is essentially what legalizers suggest. With all the other problems we face, it seems absurd to legalize something that in turn could destroy us.

Organizations to Contact

The editors have compiled the following list of organizations concerned with the issues debated in this book. The descriptions are derived from materials provided by the organizations. All have publications or information available for interested readers. The list was compiled on the date of publication of the present volume; the information provided here may change. Be aware that many organizations take several weeks or longer to respond to inquiries, so allow as much time as possible.

American Civil Liberties Union (ACLU)
125 Broad St., 18th Floor, New York, NY 10004-2400
(212) 549-2500
e-mail: aclu@aclu.org • website: www.aclu.org

The ACLU is a national organization that works to defend Americans' civil rights guaranteed by the U.S. Constitution. It provides legal defense, research, and education. The ACLU opposes the criminal prohibition of marijuana and the civil liberties violations that result from it. Its publications include *ACLU Briefing Paper #19: Against Drug Prohibition* and *Ira Glasser on Marijuana Myths and Facts.*

American Council for Drug Education (ACDE)
164 W. 74th St., New York, NY 10023
(800) 488-DRUG ext. 3784 • fax: (212) 595-2553
website: www.acde.org

The American Council for Drug Education informs the public about the harmful effects of abusing drugs and alcohol. It gives the public access to scientifically based, compelling prevention programs and materials. ACDE has resources for parents, youth, educators, prevention professionals, employers, health care professionals, and other concerned community members who are working to help America's youth avoid the dangers of drug and alcohol abuse.

Cato Institute
1000 Massachusetts Ave. NW, Washington, DC 20001-5403
(202) 842-0200 • fax: (202) 842-3490
e-mail: service@cato.org • website: www.cato.org

The institute is a public policy research foundation dedicated to limiting the control of government and to protecting individual liberty. Cato, which strongly favors drug legalization, publishes the *Cato Journal* three times a year and the *Cato Policy Report* bimonthly.

Committees of Correspondence
11 John St., Room 506, New York, NY 10038
(212) 233-7151 • fax: (212) 233-7063

The Committees of Correspondence is a national coalition of community groups that campaign against drug abuse among youth by publishing data about drugs and drug abuse. The coalition opposes drug legalization and advocates treatment for drug abusers. Its publications include the quarterly *Drug Abuse Newsletter*, the periodic *Drug Prevention Resource Manual*, and related pamphlets, brochures, and article reprints.

Drug Enforcement Administration (DEA)
2401 Jefferson Davis Highway, Alexandria, VA 22301
website: www.usdoj.gov/dea

The DEA is the federal agency charged with enforcing the nation's drug laws. The agency concentrates on stopping the smuggling and distribution of narcotics in the United States and abroad. It publishes the *Drug Enforcement Magazine* three times a year.

Drug Policy Foundation
4455 Connecticut Ave. NW, Suite B500, Washington, DC 20008-2328
(202) 537-5005 • fax: (202) 537-3007
e-mail: dpf@dpf.org • website:www.dpf.org

The foundation supports the creation of drug policies that respect individual rights, protect community health, and minimize the involvement of the criminal justice system. It supports legalizing many drugs and increasing the number of treatment programs for addicts. Publications include the bimonthly *Drug Policy Letter* and the book *The Great Drug War*. It also distributes *Press Clips*, an annual compilation of newspaper articles on drug legalization issues, as well as legislative updates.

Family Research Council
801 G St. NW, Washington, DC 20001
(202) 393-2100 • fax: (202) 393-2134
e-mail: corrdept@frc.org • website: www.frc.org

The council analyzes issues affecting the family and seeks to ensure that the interests of the traditional family are considered in the formulation of public policy. It lobbies legislatures and promotes public debate on issues concerning the family. The council publishes articles and position papers against the legalization of medicinal marijuana.

Financial Crimes Enforcement Network (FinCEN)
2070 Chain Bridge Rd., Suite 200, Vienna, VA 22182
(703) 905-3770 • fax: (703) 905-3885
e-mail: webmaster@fincen.treas.gov • website: www.treas.gov/fincen

A bureau of the Treasury Department, FinCEN works to support and strengthen international and domestic antimoney laundering efforts. To foster interagency and global cooperation, FinCEN provides information, analysis, and technological assistance. Its publications include the *Global Fight Against Money Laundering* and the *FinCEN Advisory*, which provides information on approaches to combating money laundering.

Heritage Foundation
214 Massachusetts Ave. NE, Washington, DC 20002-2302
(202) 546-4400
e-mail: info@heritage.org • website: www.heritage.org

The Heritage Foundation is a conservative public policy research institute that opposes the legalization of drugs and advocates strengthening law enforcement to stop drug abuse. It publishes position papers on a broad range of topics, including drug issues. Its regular publications include the monthly *Policy Review*, the *Backgrounder* series of occasional papers, and the *Heritage Lecture* series.

Join Together
441 Stuart St., 7th Floor, Boston, MA 02116
(617) 437-1500 • fax: (617) 437-9394
e-mail: info@jointogether.org • website: www.jointogether.org

Founded in 1991, Join Together supports community-based efforts to reduce, prevent, and treat substance abuse. It publishes community action kits to facilitate grassroots efforts to increase awareness of substance abuse issues as well as a quarterly newsletter.

Lindesmith Center
925 Ninth Ave., New York, NY 10019
(212) 548-0695 • fax: (212) 548-4670
website: www.lindesmith.org

The Lindesmith Center and Drug Policy Foundation, two major drug policy organizations, merged on July 1, 2000, and became TLC-DPF. TLC-DPF seeks to educate Americans and others about alternatives to current drug policies on issues ranging from marijuana and adolescent drug use to illicit drug addiction, the spread of infectious diseases, policing drug markets, and alternatives to incarceration. It addresses issues of drug policy reform through a variety of projects, including the International Harm Reduction Development (IHRD), a response to increased drug use and HIV transmissions in eastern Europe. The center also publishes fact sheets on topics such as needle and syringe availability, drug prohibition and the U.S. prison system, and drug education.

Marijuana Policy Project
PO Box 77492-Capitol Hill, Washington, DC 20013
(202) 462-5747 • fax: (202) 232-0442
e-mail: mpp@mpp.org • website: www.mpp.org

The Marijuana Policy Project develops and promotes policies to minimize the harm associated with marijuana. It is the only organization that is solely concerned with lobbying to reform the marijuana laws on the federal level. The project increases public awareness through speaking engagements, educational seminars, the mass media, and briefing papers.

Multidisciplinary Association for Psychedelic Studies (MAPS)
2121 Commonwealth Ave., Suite 220, Charlotte, NC 28205
(941) 924-6277 • fax: (941) 924-6265
e-mail: info@maps.org • website: www.maps.org

MAPS is a membership-based research and educational organization. It focuses on the development of beneficial, socially sanctioned uses of psychedelic drugs and marijuana. MAPS helps scientific researchers obtain governmental approval for funding on psychedelic research in human volunteers. It publishes the quarterly *MAPS Bulletin* as well as various reports and newsletters.

Narcotic Educational Foundation of America (NEFA)
28245 Crocker Ave., Suite 230, Santa Clarita, CA 91355-1201
(661) 775-6968 • fax: (661) 775-1648
e-mail: membership@cnoa.org • website: www.cnoa.org/NEFA.htm

The Narcotic Educational Foundation of America was founded in 1924 to educate the public about the dangers of drug abuse. NEFA publishes pamphlets on such subjects as glue sniffing, cocaine, alcohol, amphetamines, heroin, and drug addiction, emphasizing the effects and dangers of drugs. A series of Student Reference Sheets on drugs is distributed, including: *Barbiturates, Anabolic Steroids, Drug Dependence, Drugs and the Automotive Age, Inhalants, PCP, Prescription Drugs, Marijuana*, and *Tobacco*.

National Center on Addiction and Substance Abuse at Columbia University (CASA)
633 Third Ave., 19th Floor, New York, NY 10017
(212) 841-5200 • fax: (212) 956-8020
website: www.casacolumbia.org

CASA is a private nonprofit organization that works to educate the public about the costs and hazards of substance abuse and the prevention and treatment of all forms of chemical dependency. The center supports treatment as the best way to reduce drug addiction. It produces publications describing the harmful effects of alcohol and drug addiction and effective ways to address the problem of substance abuse.

National Clearinghouse for Alcohol and Drug Information
PO Box 2345, Rockville, MD 20847-2345
(800) 729-6686 • fax: (301) 468-6433
e-mail: shs@health.org • website: www.health.org

The clearinghouse distributes publications of the U.S. Department of Health and Human Services, the National Institute on Drug Abuse, and other federal agencies concerned with alcohol and drug abuse. Brochure titles include *Tips for Teens About Marijuana*.

National Institute on Drug Abuse (NIDA)
6001 Executive Blvd., Room 5213, Bethesda, MD 20892-9561
(301) 443-6245
e-mail: information@lists.nida.nih.gov • website: www.nida.nih.gov

NIDA supports and conducts research on drug abuse—including the yearly *Monitoring the Future Survey*—to improve addiction prevention, treatment, and policy efforts. It publishes the bimonthly *NIDA Notes* newsletter, the periodic *NIDA Capsules* fact sheets, and a catalog of research reports and public education materials, such as *Marijuana: Facts for Teens* and *Marijuana: Facts Parents Need to Know*.

National Organization for the Reform of Marijuana Laws (NORML)
1001 Connecticut Ave. NW, Suite 710, Washington, DC 20036
(202) 483-5500 • fax: (202) 483-0057
e-mail: natlnorml@aol.com • website: www.norml.org

NORML fights to legalize marijuana and to help those who have been convicted and sentenced for possessing or selling marijuana. In addition to pamphlets and position papers, it publishes the newsletter *Marijuana Highpoints*, the bimonthly *Legislative Bulletin* and *Freedom@NORML*, and the monthly *Potpourri*.

Office of National Drug Control Policy (ONDCP)
PO Box 6000, Rockville, MD 20849-6000
e-mail: ondcp@ncjrs.org • website: www.whitehousedrugpolicy.gov

The Office of National Drug Control Policy is responsible for formulating the government's national drug strategy and the president's antidrug policy as well as coordinating the federal agencies responsible for stopping drug trafficking. Drug policy studies are available upon request.

Partnership for a Drug-Free America
405 Lexington Ave., Suite 1601, New York, NY 10174
(212) 922-1560 • fax: (212) 922-1570
website: www.drugfreeamerica.org

The Partnership for a Drug-Free America is a nonprofit organization that utilizes media communication to reduce demand for illicit drugs in America. Best known for its national antidrug advertising campaign, the partnership works to "unsell" drugs to children and to prevent drug use among kids. It publishes the annual *Partnership News-letter* as well as monthly press releases about current events with which the partnership is involved.

RAND Distribution Services
1700 Main St., PO Box 2138, Santa Monica, CA 90407-2138
(310) 451-7002 • fax: (310) 451-6915
website: www.rand.org

The RAND Corporation is a research institution that seeks to improve public policy through research and analysis. RAND's Drug Policy Research Center publishes information on the costs, prevention, and treatment of alcohol and drug abuse as well as on trends in drug-law enforcement. Its extensive list of publications includes the book *Sealing the Borders* by Peter Reuter.

Reason Foundation
3415 S. Sepulveda Blvd., Suite 400, Los Angeles, CA 90034
(310) 391-2245 • fax: (310) 391-4395
e-mail: gpassantino@reason.org • website: www.reason.org

This public policy organization researches contemporary social and political problems and promotes libertarian philosophy and free-market principles. It publishes the monthly *Reason* magazine, which contains articles and editorials critical of the war on drugs and smoking regulation.

Bibliography

Books

Dan Baum
Smoke and Mirrors: The War on Drugs and the Politics of Failure. United Kingdom: Little, Brown, 1997.

Ron Chepesiuk
Hard Target: The United States' War Against International Drug Trafficking, 1982–1997. Jefferson, NC: McFarland, 1998.

Alexander Cockburn and Jeffrey St. Clair
Whiteout: The CIA, Drugs, and the Press. Monroe, ME: Common Courage Press, 1998.

Robert H. Dowd
The Enemy Is Us: How to Defeat Drug Abuse and End the War on Drugs. Gulf Breeze, FL: Hefty Press, 1997.

Dirk Chase Eldredge
Ending the War on Drugs. Bridgehampton, NY: Bridge Works, 2000.

H. Richard Friman
Narcodiplomacy: Exporting the U.S. War on Drugs. New York: Cornell University Press, 1996.

Francis Fukuyama
The Great Disruption: Human Nature and the Reconstitution of Social Order. New York: Free Press, 1999.

William C. Gilmore and Alastair N. Brown
Drug Trafficking and the Chemical Industry. Edinburgh, Scotland: Edinburgh University Press, 1997.

James P. Gray
Why Our Drug Laws Have Failed and What We Can Do About It: A Judicial Indictment of the War on Drugs. Philadelphia: Temple University Press, 2001.

Mike Gray
Drug Crazy: How We Got into This Mess and How We Can Get Out. New York: Random House, 1998.

Bruce A. Jacobs and James F. Short
Dealing Crack: The Social World of Street Corner Selling. Boston: Northeastern University Press, 1999.

Jill Jonnes
Hep-Cats, Narcs, and Pipe Dreams: A History of America's Romance with Illegal Drugs. Baltimore: Johns Hopkins University Press, 1999.

Michael Massing
The Fix. New York: Simon and Schuster, 1998.

Kathryn Meyer and Terry M. Parssinen	*Webs of Smoke: Smugglers, Warlords, Spies, and the History of the International Drug Trade.* Lanham, MD: Rowman and Littlefield, 1998.
Jillian Powell, Rob Shone, and Flick Killerby	*Drug Trafficking.* Brookfield, CT: Millbrook Press, 1997.
Kevin Jack Riley	*Snow Job? The War Against International Drug Trafficking.* Somerset, NJ: Transaction, 1996.
Thomas Sheehan, Manuel Gonzales, and Kevin McEnery	*America's Habit: Drug Abuse, Drug Trafficking, and Organized Crime.* Collington, PA: Diane Publishing, 1998.
Paul B. Stares	*Global Habit: The Drug Problem in a Borderless World.* Washington, DC: Brookings Institution Press, 1996.
Gary Webb	*Dark Alliance: The CIA, the Contras, and the Crack Cocaine Explosion.* New York: Seven Stories Press, 1999.

Periodicals

John Ward Anderson and William Branigin	"Border Trafficking," *Washington Post National Weekly Edition*, January 5, 1998. Available from PO Box 37167, Boone, IA 50037-2167.
Daniel K. Benjamin	"Devolving the Drug War," *Liberty*, January 1999. Available from PO Box 1181, Port Townsend, WA 98368.
Eva Bertram and Kenneth Sharpe	"The Drug War Corrupts Absolutely," *Los Angeles Times*, October 4, 1998. Available from 202 W. 1st St., Los Angeles, CA 90012.
Donald J. Boudreaux	"Break This Vile Addiction," *Freeman*, September 1999. Available from the Foundation for Economic Education, 30 S. Broadway, Irvington, NY 10533.
Ron Chepesiuk	"The Error of Eradication," *Toward Freedom*, February 2000.
Kevin Clarke	"Just Say No to This Drug War," *U.S. Catholic*, January 2001.
Alexander Cockburn	"The Drug War: A War on Poor, Lower Classes," *Los Angeles Times*, June 11, 1998.
Phillip Coffin	"Coca Eradication," *Foreign Policy in Focus*, October 1998.
Russell Crandall	"Colombia's Military Prospects Are Not Getting Any Brighter," *Wall Street Journal*, October 27, 2000.
Jamie Dettmer	"U.S. Drug Warriors Knock on Heaven's Door," *Insight*, April 21, 1997. Available from PO Box 91022, Washington, DC 20090-1022.
Joseph D. Douglass	"Drugs and Dollars," *New American*, April 10, 2000. Available from PO Box 8040, Appleton, WI 54912.
William Norman Grigg	"Battle Lines in the Drug War," *New American*, October 27, 1997.

Bibliography

Edward Hammond	"Biological Weapons in the Drug War?" *Z Magazine*, November 1999.
Patrick Lloyd Hatcher	"The Unwinnable War on the Drug Trade," *Orbis*, Fall 1997.
John Hightower	"Our Tax Billions Go to Losing a War in Colombia," *Hightower Lowdown*, July 2000. Available from PO Box 20511, New York, NY 10009-9991.
William F. Jasper	"A Narco-Vietnam," *New American*, April 24, 2000.
Bill Masters	"Telling the Truth About Drug Prohibition," *Liberty*, November 2000. Available from PO Box 1181, Port Townsend, WA 98368.
Barry McCaffrey	"Legalizing Drugs Would Hurt the American Public," *Washington Post*, June 24, 1999. Available from PO Box 37167, Boone, IA 50037-2167.
Barry McCaffrey	"We Have No War on Drugs," *World & I*, February 2000. Available from the *Washington Times*, 3600 New York Ave. NE, Washington, DC 20002.
Nancy Norell	"'Asset Forfeiture' Has Deep Roots, Troubling Implications," *Gun News Digest*, Spring 1999. Available from PO Box 488, Buffalo, NY 14209.
Kelly Patricia O'Meara	"Dirty Dollars," *Insight*, May 15, 2000.
William Raynor	"Coca and NAFTA," *Toward Freedom*, June/July 1997.
Helen Redmond	"The War on Drugs: Myth and Reality," *International Socialist Review*, December 2000–January 2001.
Bill Ritter	"Fighting the Real War on Drugs," *World & I*, February 2000.
John S. Robey	"The Deconstitutionalized Zone," *Liberty*, March 1999.
Larry Rohter	"Ecuador Afraid as a Drug War Heads Its Way," *The New York Times*, January 8, 2001.
Roberto Suro	"From the Border to the Neighborhood," *Washington Post National Weekly Edition*, January 19, 1998.
Suzanne Timmons and Cristina Lindblad	"Cocaine Crusade or Dirty War?" *Business Week*, December 6, 1999.
Eric A. Voth	"America's Longest 'War,'" *World & I*, February 2000.

Index